From Apathy to Activism

Building Sustained Engagement for the Public Good

From Apathy to Activism

Building Sustained Engagement for the Public Good

From Apathy to Activism:
Building Sustained Engagement for the Public Good

Second Edition

Richard Rawson, Psy.D., MBA

© 2025 Richard Rawson
All rights reserved.

No part of this book may be reproduced, stored, or transmitted in any form or by any means without the prior written permission of the author, except for brief quotations used in reviews or scholarly works.

This book is intended for educational and informational purposes only. It does not constitute professional, legal, or clinical advice.

ISBN: 979-8-9878416-9-3

Published by Rawson Internet Marketing.
United States of America.

Note on the Second Edition

This second edition does not change the direction of the book. It tightens the reins. The question at its center remains the same: how people move from disengagement toward meaningful participation in public life. What has changed is the attention given to what allows that participation to last—and what it must withstand.

In revising this edition, the focus shifts away from motivation as a spark and toward the conditions that make continued involvement possible. Less emphasis is placed on urgency as a driver. More is given to limits, structure, judgment, and the adjustments required when engagement meets resistance, delay, or power.

This revision reflects a clearer understanding of how engagement actually unfolds. Participation rarely moves in a straight line. It proceeds unevenly—through action and pause, effort and recalibration, visibility and obscurity. Engagement now happens across fragmented intervals: through reading, listening, returning, and re-entering rather than through a single, uninterrupted arc.

The structure of this edition reflects that reality. Sections are designed to stand on their own while contributing to a longer progression, allowing understanding to deepen even when attention is partial or disrupted.

Several sections have been pared back. Others have been reworked to speak more directly to what happens after initial momentum fades—when enthusiasm collides with limits, when institutions resist clarity, and when persistence becomes more important than intensity.

Readers familiar with the first edition may notice these changes. New readers may simply encounter a steadier guide—grounded less in momentum than in continuity, and less in hope than in clarity.

Preface

Most people don't tune out because they don't care. They tune out because the problems feel too large, too tangled, and too far removed from anything they can actually influence. When every issue arrives framed as a crisis, it becomes difficult to know where to stand—let alone what to do. So people wait. They watch. They argue quietly about causes and blame while the machinery keeps moving. That waiting carries a cost.

This book grew out of that space between caring and acting. The distance between knowing something matters and believing your effort matters enough to make a difference. Large problems rarely begin that way. They start small. They start close to home. They grow because enough people decide it's someone else's responsibility to stop them. This book is about what happens when that assumption breaks down.

The stories here are not about professional activists or grand gestures. They are about ordinary people who stepped forward because the alternative—doing nothing—began to feel heavier than the risk of acting.

Citizens who fought to preserve public access to the Rhode Island shoreline when powerful interests tried to close it off, and succeeded. A resident who turned an abandoned city lot into a working community garden, not to make a statement, but because the neighborhood needed it. None of these people set out to change the world. They set out to change something they could see.

Democratic life does not run on good intentions alone. It endures when people choose to participate—sometimes clumsily, sometimes imperfectly, but deliberately. One person rarely shifts the ground by themselves. Momentum is built through a series of small decisions, repeated over time.

This book is not a call to outrage or ideology. It is an examination of why people disengage, and what helps them re-engage in ways that can be sustained. Drawing on psychology, sociology, anthropology, and neuroscience, *From Apathy to Activism* looks at the forces that move people from observation to involvement. It focuses on what supports participation once the initial impulse fades: how to navigate resistance, manage limits, and act without burning out or losing perspective.

At its core, the book is about shifting—how insight becomes behavior, and how small actions begin to matter when they are repeated, shared, and allowed to compound. You do not need to become someone else to act. You do not need permission, credentials, or a perfect plan. What you need is clarity, steadiness, and a willingness to step out of the audience.

If you have ever felt frustrated by inaction—your own or others'—this book is written for you. Not to stir emotion, but to help you understand where influence actually begins. Change starts quietly, when someone decides not to sit this one out. That is the shift this book is about.

Table of Contents

Chapter 1: The Anatomy of Apathy 1

Chapter 2: From Apathy to Empathy 15

Chapter 3: From Empathy to Engagement 21

Chapter 4: From Engagement to Advocacy 29

Chapter 5: From Individual Advocacy to Collective Action . . 37

Chapter 6: Staying Oriented in an Information Environment . 47

Chapter 7: Difference, Inclusion, and Collective Intelligence . 57

Chapter 8: Division, Conflict, and the Work of Repair 67

Chapter 9: When Engagement Produces More Than Intended . 77

Chapter 10: Grassroots Organizing 87

Chapter 11: A Change-Maker's Guide 95

Chapter 12: From Practice to Perspective 105

Table of Contents

CHAPTER 1
The Anatomy of Apathy

THE ANATOMY OF APATHY

Section 1

Apathy as a Pattern of Withdrawal

Apathy is not a lack of caring. It is a pattern of withdrawal that develops when demands outpace capacity. Most people do not wake up intending to disengage from the world around them. They arrive there gradually—through overload, disappointment, and the repeated experience of caring without seeing results. Over time, concern begins to feel optional. Action starts to feel naïve.

That is how apathy takes hold. At a societal level, it appears as indifference to problems everyone knows exist but few feel responsible for addressing. Corruption becomes background noise. Climate change turns into an abstract debate. Injustice is acknowledged, then postponed. The result is not outrage, but paralysis.

At a personal level, apathy looks different but comes from the same place. People lose interest in shaping their own lives. Decisions are deferred. Responsibility is minimized. This form of disengagement often grows out of past failure, chronic stress, depression, or the sense that effort no longer pays off.

These two forms—personal and societal—are not separate. They reinforce one another. When individuals feel powerless, societies stagnate. When societies normalize disengagement, individuals retreat further.

The common thread is helplessness—the belief that one person's actions amount to little more than a drop in the ocean. Once that belief takes hold, withdrawal begins to feel reasonable. History suggests otherwise.

Few moments illustrate the cost of apathy more clearly than the 1964 murder of Kitty Genovese in New York City. As she was attacked outside her apartment, multiple neighbors heard her cries. Most assumed someone else would act. Some misread the situation. Others chose not to get involved.

No single failure caused her death. Collective inaction did. The case prompted decades of research into what psychologists later called the bystander effect—the tendency for individuals to avoid responsibility when others are present. When responsibility is shared, it often dissolves.

A related finding emerged from the Good Samaritan experiment, which showed that people are less likely to help someone in distress when they are rushed, distracted, or mentally overloaded. Good intentions do not disappear under pressure. They are crowded out.

These findings matter because they reveal something uncomfortable: apathy is not always the result of bad character. It is often the product of context, pace, and perceived futility. That does not excuse inaction—but it helps explain it. The danger arises when apathy hardens into habit.

When withdrawal becomes routine, responsibility shifts outward by default. People begin to assume that someone else—an institution, a leader, a system—will intervene. Over time, disengagement stops feeling like a choice and starts to feel like common sense.

The next sections examine how that withdrawal spreads beyond individuals, shaping how responsibility diffuses when problems grow large and impersonal.

Section 2

When Responsibility Diffuses at Scale

The patterns revealed by the bystander effect and the Good Samaritan experiment do not stop at street corners or laboratory settings. They appear wherever problems grow large enough that responsibility begins to feel distant.

The same forces that keep people from stepping in during a crisis also shape how societies respond to long-term challenges. When issues expand in scope and complexity, individual effort can start to feel insignificant. Responsibility shifts upward—toward governments, corporations, institutions—while personal involvement recedes.

Climate change offers a clear example. Most people understand that it is real and serious. Hesitation emerges not from doubt, but from scale. When a problem spans continents and generations, individual action begins to feel symbolic rather than effective. People assume that others are better positioned to act, and that their own role is marginal. This is diffusion of responsibility operating at a societal level.

A similar pattern appears with racism and inequality. Many people recognize injustice when they see it. What is less clear is how they are meant to respond in a way that feels proportionate and meaningful. Uncertainty leads to hesitation. Hesitation gives way to silence. Over time, silence begins to feel like a reasonable position. It is not.

The Good Samaritan experiment adds another layer of explanation. Even when people care, action competes with pressure, distraction, and fatigue. When attention is divided and demands accumulate, intention alone is rarely enough. Engagement is postponed, often indefinitely, under the assumption that conditions will improve later. They rarely do.

Understanding these dynamics reframes the problem. The issue is not a lack of concern. It is that concern does not reliably translate into action without clear paths forward.

When disengagement grows out of uncertainty and overload, progress depends less on louder appeals and more on practical entry points. Defined roles. Manageable steps. Evidence that effort leads somewhere.

People are more likely to act when responsibility is specific, when the cost feels reasonable, and when participation fits into the reality of daily life. Remove those conditions, and even thoughtful, well-intentioned people step back.

This is where individual agency reappears—not as heroism, but as participation. Progress does not require everyone to do everything. It requires enough people to do something they can sustain. The research points to a simple conclusion: people engage when action feels possible.

The next section looks more closely at the conditions that quietly discourage action, even when concern is present.

Section 3

Conditions That Discourage Action

People do not avoid action because they lack values. More often, they step back because the conditions surrounding action make involvement feel risky, confusing, or futile. Before participation can increase, those conditions have to be understood. What follows is not a list of excuses. It is a map of the forces that quietly steer people away from involvement—even when concern is present.

Limited Awareness: Information is not evenly distributed. Some people do not see certain issues clearly, either because they have never been exposed to them or because the information they encounter is partial, distorted, or contradictory. When understanding is incomplete, urgency rarely forms. What is not clearly understood seldom feels personal.

Distance From the Problem: Problems feel less pressing when they appear far away—geographically, socially, or temporally. If an issue does not seem to touch daily life, concern is easily postponed. Climate change is often framed as something that will matter later, somewhere else. That framing dulls the sense that action is needed now. Distance lowers pressure. Pressure drives action.

Feeling Outmatched: Large problems intimidate. When an issue appears vast and entrenched, people question whether effort is worth the cost. The gap between individual action and systemic scale makes participation feel symbolic rather than effective. This sense of futility halts more action than disagreement ever could.

Economic Pressure: For many people, survival comes first. When work is unstable or resources are scarce, broader social issues fall down the priority list. Speaking out can feel like a luxury—or a risk that cannot be absorbed. This reflects constraint, not indifference.

Cultural Conditioning: Every culture carries assumptions about what is normal, acceptable, or worth challenging. Longstanding beliefs—about gender, race, class, or authority—shape how people interpret injustice. When a norm has gone unquestioned for generations, challenging it can feel disruptive rather than necessary.

Ideological Filters: Political identity acts as a lens. It shapes which problems people acknowledge, which solutions they consider legitimate, and which voices they trust. Once an issue becomes entangled with ideology, discussion narrows and positions harden. Dialogue gives way to alignment. Progress slows.

Social Pressure: Most people do not decide in isolation. They take cues from peers, workplaces, families, and communities. When speaking up carries social cost, silence becomes the safer option. Conformity does not require agreement. It only requires hesitation.

Structural Constraints: Some barriers are not psychological at all. They are structural. Inequality, discrimination, and institutional bias limit who has the time, energy, and access needed to participate. When systems are uneven, engagement becomes harder for those already carrying the most weight.

Absence of Direction: Action without direction rarely lasts. When leadership is unclear or fragmented, people struggle to see where their effort fits. Without momentum or coordination, participation fades. People do not need charismatic heroes. They need clarity.

Media Saturation: Media shapes attention. When issues are ignored, they disappear from public awareness. When they are sensationalized, people burn out. Constant exposure without context or progress leads to disengagement, not commitment. Noise replaces understanding.

Fear of Consequences: Action carries risk. Speaking out can affect employment, relationships, and personal safety. For many, the potential cost outweighs the uncertain benefit. Silence becomes a form of self-protection. Fear does not negate conviction. It restrains it.

Social Disorientation: Periods of rapid change unsettle norms. When expectations shift faster than people can adapt, uncertainty grows. In that uncertainty, people hesitate, unsure which actions will help and which will backfire. Confusion breeds passivity.

Weak Sense of Belonging: People are more likely to act when they feel connected to a cause or a group. When movements feel exclusive, abstract, or misaligned with personal identity, participation drops. Belonging precedes commitment.

Competing Priorities: Everyone ranks obligations. When personal advancement, comfort, or security take precedence, collective concerns recede. This is not always selfishness. It is often habit reinforced over time. Values do not disappear. They are crowded out.

None of these conditions operate in isolation. They overlap, reinforce one another, and create a persistent drag on action. Understanding them does not solve the problem—but it does change where effort is best applied. Barriers cannot be reduced if they are not recognized. Action cannot be expected without accounting for the conditions people are navigating.

The next section turns inward, examining how mindset shapes whether people stay engaged once these pressures are encountered.

Section 4

Mindset and the Willingness to Stay Engaged

Action does not begin with outrage. It begins with how people interpret effort, difficulty, and possibility. Some people treat challenges as signals to engage. Others interpret the same challenges as evidence that nothing will change. The difference often lies not in values, but in mindset.

Psychologist Carol Dweck describes two broad ways people understand ability and limitation. A growth mindset assumes that skills, judgment, and effectiveness develop through effort and experience. A fixed mindset assumes they are largely set from the outset. That distinction matters for sustained engagement.

People with a growth mindset do not expect to get everything right. They anticipate learning as part of participation. Setbacks are interpreted as feedback rather than failure. Effort is not a sign of inadequacy. It is a condition of progress.

Applied to social action, this outlook makes continued involvement more likely. Problems are not viewed as permanent states. They are treated as ongoing challenges—difficult, uneven, and responsive to persistence and adjustment over time.

A fixed mindset leads in a different direction. When people believe outcomes are predetermined, or that only experts and institutions can make a difference, participation begins to feel futile. Challenges are avoided. Feedback is dismissed. The progress of others feels discouraging rather than instructive. In that frame, disengagement appears rational.

Research on mindset was not designed to explain activism directly, but the implications are consistent. Studies link a growth mindset with resilience, problem-solving, empathy, and sustained effort—qualities that matter when change is slow and resistance is common.

One study published in Child Development found that adolescents with a growth mindset were more likely to respond constructively to social problems rather than withdraw from them. Other research suggests that teaching a growth mindset can reduce aggression and increase prosocial behavior, particularly in situations involving conflict or frustration. None of this guarantees action. But it changes the odds.

Mindset does not determine values. It shapes how values survive contact with difficulty. People do not disengage because problems are hard. They disengage when difficulty is interpreted as futility. A growth mindset interrupts that interpretation. It reframes effort as investment rather than waste.

This shift does not require optimism. It requires patience and tolerance for imperfection.

Social change is rarely clean. It involves trial, correction, and persistence. Those willing to remain engaged long enough to learn are the ones most likely to matter. Activism does not demand certainty. It demands the belief that learning is still possible.

The next section looks at how cognitive bias—particularly the tendency to focus on threat and loss—can quietly undermine that belief, even among people who care.

Section 5

How Negativity Bias Narrows Participation

Human attention is not evenly balanced. Threats register faster than opportunities. Losses linger longer than gains. A single negative outcome can outweigh several positive ones.

Psychologists refer to this tendency as negativity bias—the inclination to give greater weight to negative experiences, information, and possibilities. It is not a flaw. It is a survival adaptation.

For most of human history, heightened sensitivity to danger improved the odds of survival. Missing a threat carried a higher cost than missing a benefit. That imbalance shaped how memory forms, how attention is allocated, and how judgment operates.

Negative events leave deeper impressions. They are remembered more vividly and revisited more often. Their influence persists long after the original moment has passed.

Negativity bias does not disappear in modern life. It adapts. At a personal level, it can narrow perspective. Criticism is replayed more readily than praise. Failure is anticipated more quickly than success. Risk begins to feel heavier than reward. Over time, initiative gives way to caution. At a societal level, the effect compounds.

Threat-focused narratives dominate attention. Fear spreads faster than reassurance. Media coverage gravitates toward conflict and breakdown—not because progress is absent, but because danger captures attention more reliably than stability.

In public discourse, negativity bias is often used deliberately. Fear-based messaging mobilizes quickly. Alarm travels farther than explanation. The short-term effect may be engagement. The long-term effect is fatigue. This matters for participation.

Negativity bias can initiate action. Injustice, environmental damage, and abuses of power often provoke strong responses precisely because they violate expectations of safety or fairness. That emotional charge can move people to act. But the same bias can also limit progress.

When attention is fixed solely on what is broken—without credible paths forward—people disengage. Prolonged exposure to crisis without agency leads not to urgency, but to withdrawal. Outrage without traction turns into resignation.

Negativity bias also shapes how groups view one another. When attention locks onto the worst behavior of perceived opponents, divisions harden. Dialogue narrows. Positions turn into identities. Cooperation becomes suspect.

None of this means negativity bias should be avoided. It means it must be understood. People are motivated not only by hope, but by the desire to prevent loss. Framing action around avoiding concrete harm can be effective—when paired with clear, attainable steps. The danger lies in stopping at alarm.

Awareness alters how bias operates. When people recognize their tendency to fixate on threat, they regain some control over how information shapes judgment. When movements balance urgency with agency, concern becomes sustainable rather than exhausting.

Negativity bias does not determine outcomes. But left unchecked, it quietly steers behavior toward fear, division, and eventual disengagement. Used deliberately, it can focus attention. Used carelessly, it can stall the very change it is meant to provoke.

How Negativity Bias Manifests in Everyday Behavior: Negativity bias rarely presents itself as pessimism. More often, it appears as avoidance. When people perceive risk—social, emotional, cognitive, or practical—the mind looks for ways to reduce exposure. Sometimes that means disengaging. Sometimes it means blending in. Sometimes it means waiting for someone else to go first. The behaviors that follow are not random. They are patterned responses to perceived threat.

Apathy, diffusion of responsibility, conformity, situational hesitation, and mental overload are not separate failures of character. They are different expressions of the same underlying calculation: the perceived cost of acting exceeds the perceived cost of not acting. Understanding that calculation matters. Once it is visible, these responses stop looking like indifference and begin to look like self-protection.

Apathy as a Withdrawal Response: Apathy is often mistaken for a lack of concern. More accurately, it is a withdrawal response. When attention is repeatedly drawn to failure, conflict, or scale without resolution, emotional investment becomes costly. Distance offers relief. Over time, that distance hardens. People disengage not because they misunderstand the stakes, but because constant exposure to threat without agency feels unsustainable. Apathy is not emptiness. It is fatigue that has learned to resemble neutrality.

Diffusion of Responsibility: Negativity bias heightens sensitivity to risk, including social risk. When acting alone feels exposed, responsibility is unconsciously shifted outward. In groups, this appears as waiting. When many people are present, each individual feels less pressure to absorb the cost of acting.

Responsibility does not disappear. It disperses. This diffusion reduces personal risk, but it also reduces the likelihood that anyone intervenes. The safer silence becomes individually, the more dangerous it becomes collectively.

Social Influence and Conformity: Under uncertainty, people look to others for cues. Negativity bias amplifies fear of judgment, rejection, and isolation. As a result, conformity begins to feel safer than dissent, even when private beliefs differ from public behavior. Group norms become signals of acceptable risk. Standing apart feels costly. Blending in feels prudent. Conviction is not erased. Expression is restrained.

Situational Constraint: Context shapes behavior more than intention. Under financial pressure, time scarcity, or personal stress, attention narrows. Immediate threats and obligations take precedence. Broader concerns recede—not because they no longer matter, but because mental bandwidth contracts. Negativity bias prioritizes what feels urgent over what feels important. Action becomes situational rather than value-driven.

Cognitive Load: When the mind is saturated, engagement declines. Complex problems demand attention, evaluation, and judgment. Under high cognitive load, the brain conserves energy by avoiding additional strain. Difficult issues are postponed. Nuanced understanding gives way to simplification or avoidance. This is not laziness. It is a protective response to mental saturation. When too many threats compete for attention, inaction becomes the default.

These patterns are not flaws to be corrected through pressure or persuasion. They are signals. They indicate where perceived risk outweighs perceived agency. Where attention has been flooded without direction. Where caring feels costly and action feels exposed.

The movement from apathy toward participation begins by reversing that equation—not by demanding greater concern, but by lowering the psychological cost of engagement.

CHAPTER 2
From Apathy to Empathy

Section 1

Empathy as a Shift in Attention

Empathy is not a feeling people summon on command. It is a shift in attention. When people disengage, it is rarely because they have stopped caring altogether. More often, they have narrowed the circle of what feels close enough to matter. Empathy expands that circle—not through sentiment, but through recognition. Empathy begins when another person's situation stops being abstract.

It is easy to confuse empathy with sympathy, but the two operate differently. Sympathy acknowledges distress from a distance. It observes. Empathy closes that distance. It does not require agreement or shared experience—only the willingness to take another person's reality seriously. That distinction matters for engagement.

Sympathy can coexist with inaction. Empathy rarely does. Once a situation feels real—once the people involved are no longer interchangeable—the cost of disengagement rises. Indifference becomes harder to justify.

This is why empathy plays such a central role in the movement from apathy to action. It shifts problems out of the category of issues and into the category of people. And people are more difficult to ignore.

Empathy does not arrive all at once. It develops through exposure and attention. Listening closely to someone's experience without correcting, minimizing, or redirecting it. Encountering perspectives that do not mirror one's own. Remaining present long enough for discomfort to register rather than be deflected.

This kind of listening is not passive. It requires restraint. The impulse to fix, argue, or compare has to be set aside. What replaces it is understanding—not agreement, but clarity about what another person is navigating. That clarity changes behavior.

When people feel seen and understood, trust grows. As trust grows, cooperation becomes possible. Empathy does not simply soften attitudes. It alters how responsibility is calculated.

Empathy alone does not resolve systemic problems. But without it, those problems remain distant and negotiable. Empathy is what keeps concern from fading once attention moves elsewhere. It is not a substitute for action. It is what makes action harder to postpone.

Moving from apathy to empathy does not require becoming more emotional. It requires becoming more attentive—especially to experiences that do not immediately resemble one's own. That attentiveness is the first durable step toward engagement.

Section 2

How Empathy Is Cultivated

Empathy does not grow through instruction alone. It develops through attention, regulation, and restraint. Once empathy is understood as a capacity rather than a sentiment, the question becomes practical: what makes it easier to sustain, especially when situations are tense, unfamiliar, or emotionally charged? There is no single technique. What follows is a set of reinforcing practices that help people remain present rather than reactive.

Attention Comes First: Empathy begins with listening—but not the kind that waits for its turn to respond. Attentive listening requires suspending the impulse to interrupt, correct, or solve. It involves tracking not only what is being said, but how it is said: tone, pace, hesitation, emphasis. People do not need agreement to feel understood. They need evidence that their experience has been registered accurately. When attention is genuine, defensiveness eases. As defensiveness drops, understanding becomes possible.

Regulation Makes Attention Possible: Listening well depends on emotional steadiness. When anger, anxiety, or frustration rise, attention narrows and turns inward. Empathy collapses. Simple regulation practices interrupt that collapse by creating space between stimulus and response. Slowing the breath, grounding attention in the present moment, and pausing briefly before responding all serve the same function: they reduce reactivity enough for awareness to return. These are not wellness rituals. They are functional tools for staying engaged when withdrawal would be easier.

Awareness Without Distortion: Empathy also depends on interpretation. Unexamined thought patterns—catastrophizing, personalization, rigid assumptions—distort perception and shut down understanding. Cognitive reframing is not forced optimism. It is an effort toward accuracy. When people learn to question their first interpretation rather than defend it, they create room for complexity. That room is where empathy operates.

Exposure Builds Range: Empathy strengthens through contact. Sustained interaction, direct service, and firsthand exposure to unfamiliar circumstances collapse distance. They replace assumption with context. Volunteering, community involvement, and lived experience make abstract issues tangible. This is not charity. It is proximity. Stories serve a similar function. Fiction, memoir, and long-form narrative allow people to inhabit perspectives they may never encounter directly. Over time, this builds emotional range—the ability to hold experiences that do not mirror one's own without retreating or simplifying.

Communication Carries Empathy Forward: Empathy that cannot be expressed rarely leads to action. Clear, assertive communication allows concern to be conveyed without aggression or withdrawal. It balances honesty with respect. It replaces accusation with clarity and defensiveness with specificity. Equally important is the ability to acknowledge another person's experience without endorsing every conclusion they draw. Recognition affirms reality. It does not suspend judgment. When communication remains grounded, empathy becomes relational rather than performative.

Empathy Requires Boundaries: Sustained empathy is not limitless. Without boundaries, people absorb more emotion than they can process. Fatigue follows. Resentment accumulates. Withdrawal can look like apathy, but it is often overload. Empathy functions best when paired with discernment—knowing when to engage deeply, when to step back, and when responsibility must be shared rather than carried alone.

A Capacity That Requires Maintenance: Empathy is not a phase. It is a condition that requires upkeep. It develops unevenly, strengthens with practice, and weakens under strain. Progress is rarely linear. What matters is continuity—the willingness to return attention to others after frustration, misunderstanding, or fatigue. Empathy does not demand constant emotional openness. It requires a consistent willingness to notice. That willingness keeps concern from fading—and engagement from becoming optional.

CHAPTER 3
From Empathy to Engagement

Section 1

When Empathy Becomes Personal

Empathy becomes actionable when it stops being abstract. Concern alone does not move people. Most individuals are aware of suffering beyond their immediate surroundings. What changes behavior is not awareness, but proximity—the moment an issue intersects with daily life in a concrete way.

This is where engagement begins. When a problem appears close enough to touch—physically, socially, or relationally—it becomes harder to defer responsibility. The people involved are no longer interchangeable. The situation acquires detail, context, and consequence. Distance collapses, and with it, the comfort of detachment.

Empathy shifts at this point from observation to recognition. This shift does not require shared identity or agreement. It requires specificity. Names instead of categories. Places instead of abstractions. Familiar routines interrupted by visible need.

Once empathy becomes personal, the cost of inaction rises. Indifference is no longer neutral. It becomes a decision—one that must be actively maintained. This is why large-scale problems often fail to mobilize individuals on their own. Scale diffuses responsibility. Personal contact concentrates it.

Engagement begins when people encounter situations they cannot unsee. When the issue appears within the perimeter of ordinary life, attention lingers. Concern settles into responsibility, not because it is demanded, but because it feels unavoidable. This is not idealism. It is how human attention operates.

The sections that follow examine how proximity turns recognition into participation—and how small, local actions create the conditions for sustained involvement.

Section 2
Engagement Begins With Proximity

Engagement rarely begins with intention alone. It begins when circumstances move close enough to demand attention. Proximity can take different forms. Sometimes it is physical—a problem encountered on the way to work, in a neighborhood, or in a shared public space. Sometimes it is relational—an issue affecting someone known personally rather than at a distance. Sometimes it is temporal—the moment when delay is no longer possible.

In each case, the effect is the same. Distance collapses, and responsibility becomes harder to defer. A snow-covered sidewalk left uncleared, an abandoned lot accumulating debris, a classroom where students fall behind year after year—none of these situations are abstract. They are visible, recurring, and embedded in ordinary routines. Because they are encountered repeatedly, they resist being ignored.

These situations do not feel like causes. They feel like conditions. Proximity alters how people calculate effort. When a problem is encountered regularly, action begins to feel less like a statement and more like maintenance. Small interventions—shoveling a path, cleaning a space, staying late to help—become part of the rhythm of daily life.

This is a critical shift. When engagement is framed as maintenance rather than mobilization, it becomes more sustainable. The work is no longer performed to make a point. It is performed to keep something functioning.

Proximity also clarifies impact. Results are visible. Feedback is immediate. Effort leads to observable change, even if that change is limited in scope. This visibility reinforces participation, not through reward, but through evidence that action matters.

Importantly, proximity does not require urgency or crisis. In many cases, engagement begins precisely because a situation persists. What is repeated becomes familiar. What is familiar becomes harder to abandon.

This is why engagement often grows out of local, unremarkable settings rather than dramatic events. People act not because they are called upon, but because the situation is already part of their world. Proximity turns concern into responsibility by narrowing the gap between awareness and action.

The next section examines how repetition stabilizes that responsibility, transforming isolated responses into sustained engagement.

Section 3

Engagement Stabilizes Through Repetition

Initial action does not guarantee continued involvement. What sustains engagement is repetition. When an action is taken once, it remains a choice. When it is taken repeatedly, it begins to take on a different character. It becomes part of a routine. Responsibility settles into place not through resolve, but through familiarity.

This shift matters. Repetition lowers the psychological cost of action. What once required deliberation becomes automatic. The question is no longer whether to act, but when. Effort decreases as habit forms. Engagement stabilizes because it demands less constant justification.

Repeated action also reshapes identity, quietly and without declaration. People do not need to decide that they are "activists" or "advocates." They simply become the person who shows up, the one who takes care of something that needs attention. This is how engagement avoids burnout.

High-intensity efforts are difficult to sustain. They rely on emotion, urgency, and external reinforcement. Repetitive actions rely on rhythm. They fit into existing patterns of life. Because they do not require constant escalation, they endure.

Repetition also clarifies boundaries. When involvement continues over time, people learn what they can realistically carry and what must be shared. Expectations adjust. Effort becomes measured rather than reactive.

Importantly, repetition does not require immediate success. Many forms of engagement persist despite slow progress or partial results. What keeps them going is not optimism, but continuity. The action itself becomes worthwhile because it maintains something that would otherwise degrade.

This is why engagement often appears modest from the outside. It does not announce itself. It does not scale quickly. But it accumulates. Over time, repeated actions create stability. Stability creates reliability. Reliability attracts attention.

The next section examines how that reliability draws others in, transforming individual effort into shared responsibility.

Section 4

Individual Action Attracts Collective Effort

Collective engagement rarely begins with coordination. It begins with visibility. When someone acts consistently, others notice. Not because the action is announced, but because it becomes part of the environment. Reliability signals that something is being tended to. Over time, that signal invites attention.

This is how individual effort draws others in. People are more likely to participate when they see that involvement is already underway. The presence of an active participant reduces uncertainty. It answers practical questions before they are asked: What does this involve? How demanding is it? Does it make a difference?

Observation lowers risk. When engagement is visible and routine, participation begins to feel less like a leap and more like a step. Others join not because they are persuaded, but because the pathway is clear. They can see how effort fits into ordinary life.

This process is gradual. One person's repeated action creates a point of reference. A second person assists. A third adapts the effort to a different context. Responsibility spreads—not through diffusion, but through imitation.

Importantly, this kind of growth does not require consensus or shared ideology. People participate for different reasons. Some are motivated by concern. Others by habit, proximity, or simple availability. What they share is not belief, but behavior.

As participation expands, engagement becomes less fragile. Responsibility is distributed. Absences are absorbed. The effort no longer depends on a single individual's capacity. This is the quiet transition from individual action to shared effort.

What emerges is not a movement, but a pattern. A set of behaviors that others recognize as normal and worth sustaining. Over time, that pattern can support larger coordination—but it does not begin there. Collective engagement grows when individual action is steady enough to be trusted.

The final section identifies the common features that allow this progression—from personal involvement to shared responsibility—to hold over time.

Section 5

Patterns That Sustain Engagement

Across these examples, the pattern is consistent. Engagement does not begin with ideology, identity, or instruction. It begins when attention narrows, responsibility becomes specific, and action fits into the reality of daily life. Several conditions appear repeatedly.

First, engagement emerges through proximity. Problems that are visible, recurring, and embedded in ordinary routines resist abstraction. They remain present long enough to demand response.

Second, engagement stabilizes through repetition. Action becomes sustainable when it is woven into habit rather than driven by intensity. Repetition lowers the cost of participation and reduces reliance on emotion or urgency.

Third, engagement attracts others through reliability. When effort is consistent and visible, it signals that participation is possible without extraordinary sacrifice. Observation reduces uncertainty and invites imitation.

Fourth, engagement persists when responsibility is shared. As others join, effort becomes distributed. No single individual carries the full weight. Absence no longer collapses the work.

Finally, engagement endures when boundaries are respected. Sustainable involvement allows for limits, adjustment, and recovery. It avoids the expectation of constant availability or escalating commitment.

None of these conditions require exceptional people. They require ordinary actions under conditions that allow them to continue. This is why attempts to increase participation through pressure, persuasion, or moral appeal often fail. They focus on motivation while ignoring the structures that make engagement viable.

Engagement is not sustained by belief alone. It is sustained by design. When conditions support attention, repetition, visibility, and shared responsibility, participation becomes less fragile. It no longer depends on crisis or conviction. It becomes part of how people relate to their environment and to one another.

Chapter 3 has shown how empathy crosses into action. The chapters that follow examine how these patterns can be supported—or undermined—by larger systems and institutions

CHAPTER 4
From Engagement to Advocacy

Section 1

When Engagement Becomes Directed

Engagement becomes advocacy when attention gains direction. Up to this point, engagement has been defined by proximity, repetition, and shared effort. People respond to what they encounter. They maintain what they can see. They participate where responsibility feels close enough to carry. Advocacy begins when that participation is oriented toward a purpose that extends beyond the immediate moment.

This shift does not require escalation. It requires clarity. Directed engagement differs from reactive involvement in one essential way: it is guided by intention over time. Actions are no longer taken only because a situation is present, but because they serve a broader aim—protecting a space, improving an outcome, or advancing a condition that matters.

Advocacy is often misunderstood as louder engagement. Public protest, persuasion, and confrontation dominate popular images of advocacy. While those forms exist, they are not its foundation. Advocacy is defined less by visibility than by continuity with purpose.

In practice, this often looks understated. An individual continues showing up, but with clearer priorities. Effort is focused rather than scattered. Decisions about where to invest time and energy become deliberate. The question shifts from "What needs attention right now?" to "What deserves sustained effort?"

This distinction matters because direction stabilizes engagement. When effort is guided by purpose, participation becomes easier to maintain. Setbacks are interpreted within a longer horizon. Disappointment does not automatically signal failure. Adjustments are made without abandoning the work.

Directed engagement also introduces limits. Advocacy does not require responding to every issue or opportunity. In fact, attempting to do so often leads to dilution and fatigue. Direction provides a basis for saying no—not out of indifference, but out of proportion. This is the point where engagement matures into advocacy. Not through intensity, but through orientation.

The sections that follow examine what advocacy actually involves, how readiness develops, and how focus and sustainability are maintained over time.

Section 2

What Advocacy Actually Involves

Advocacy is often mistaken for visibility. Public statements, protests, and campaigns are the most recognizable forms, but they are not the whole of it. In many cases, they are not even the most durable. Advocacy is better understood as sustained effort directed toward a specific outcome.

At its core, advocacy involves three elements: focus, continuity, and accountability. Focus gives effort direction. Rather than responding to every issue that arises, advocacy narrows attention to a defined concern. This does not mean ignoring everything else. It means choosing where effort is most likely to matter.

Continuity gives effort weight. Advocacy is measured over time, not moments. A single action may signal concern. Repeated actions signal commitment. What distinguishes advocacy from episodic engagement is the willingness to remain involved after attention shifts elsewhere.

Accountability gives effort credibility. Advocacy accepts responsibility for outcomes, even when progress is slow or incomplete. It involves tracking whether actions are aligned with purpose and adjusting when they are not. This is not about control. It is about ownership.

Importantly, advocacy does not require persuasion at every turn. Many forms of advocacy operate quietly—through presence, maintenance, and follow-through. Some are visible. Others are relational, procedural, or structural. All are valid when they are sustained and directed.

Advocacy also differs from opinion. Holding a belief does not constitute advocacy. Expressing that belief may signal alignment, but advocacy begins when effort is invested beyond expression. Time, attention, and consistency are the currencies that turn belief into practice.

This distinction protects advocacy from performance. When effort is defined by action rather than display, it becomes harder to outsource responsibility to visibility alone. Advocacy is not measured by volume or recognition. It is measured by whether something is improved, protected, or advanced as a result of sustained involvement.

Advocacy is not reserved for experts or leaders. It emerges wherever people take responsibility for outcomes they care about and remain engaged long enough to influence them.

The next section turns inward, examining what readiness for advocacy actually entails—without assuming certainty, credentials, or permission.

Section 3

Readiness for Advocacy

Readiness for advocacy is often misunderstood as certainty. People assume they must be fully informed, emotionally resolved, or strategically prepared before taking on sustained effort. In practice, readiness rarely arrives in that form. It develops through engagement, not in advance of it.

Readiness is better understood as capacity. It involves the ability to remain involved without becoming reactive, overwhelmed, or rigid. It reflects tolerance for ambiguity, willingness to learn, and acceptance that progress is often uneven.

Advocacy does not require having all the answers. It requires the ability to stay oriented while answers evolve.

One element of readiness is understanding before acting. This does not mean exhaustive knowledge. It means taking the time to grasp the contours of an issue—who is affected, how systems operate, and where effort might have leverage. Acting without understanding often leads to misalignment and fatigue.

Another element is communication with purpose. Advocacy depends on the ability to express concern clearly and listen without defensiveness. This includes knowing when to speak, when to ask questions, and when restraint is more effective than assertion.

Equally important is self-management. Advocacy places demands on attention and emotion. Without awareness of personal limits, involvement can become unsustainable. Readiness includes recognizing signs of overload, adjusting pace, and allowing for recovery without disengaging entirely.

This is not withdrawal. It is maintenance. Readiness also involves accepting discomfort. Advocacy often brings exposure to disagreement, slow progress, and imperfect outcomes. Those experiences do not signal failure. They are part of the terrain. People who expect resolution before participation rarely remain involved long enough to influence anything.

Finally, readiness means letting go of the need for permission. Advocacy does not begin when someone is invited or authorized. It begins when responsibility is accepted for something that matters and carried forward with proportion. Readiness is not a threshold to cross. It is a capacity that develops through use.

The next section examines how focus is chosen and maintained—how engagement is directed without becoming narrow or brittle.

Section 4

Focusing Engagement Without Narrowing It

Sustained advocacy depends on focus, but focus is often misunderstood as limitation. People worry that choosing one area of engagement means abandoning others. In practice, the opposite is usually true. Focus allows effort to deepen without becoming brittle. It provides direction without closing off awareness.

Focusing engagement means deciding where responsibility can be carried realistically. This decision is shaped by proximity, capacity, and continuity. Proximity keeps effort grounded in lived conditions. Capacity determines how much can be sustained without overload. Continuity ensures that involvement can persist beyond initial interest.

When focus aligns with these factors, engagement becomes durable rather than draining. Focus also clarifies boundaries. It makes it possible to decline opportunities that do not fit without guilt or withdrawal. Saying no becomes an act of proportion rather than disengagement.

This does not mean commitment is rigid. Effective advocacy remains responsive. It adjusts as conditions change, as understanding deepens, and as others join or step back. Focus provides orientation, not confinement.

Learning plays a central role here. Advocacy rarely begins with perfect alignment. It develops through action, reflection, and adjustment. Mistakes are inevitable. What matters is the ability to recalibrate without abandoning the effort entirely.

Reflection does not require withdrawal. It requires attention. When people periodically step back to assess whether their effort is aligned with purpose and capacity, engagement strengthens. Drift is corrected. Burnout is prevented. Participation remains intentional. Focusing engagement is not about narrowing concern. It is about sustaining responsibility.

From Engagement To Advocacy

The next section examines how advocacy endures over time—how pacing, proportion, and shared responsibility protect engagement from burnout.

CHAPTER 5

From Individual Advocacy to Collective Action

FROM INDIVIDUAL ADVOCACY TO COLLECTION ACTION

Section 1

Why Collective Action Changes What's Possible

Individual advocacy matters, but it has limits. One person can protect a space, maintain a practice, or sustain attention over time. What individuals cannot easily do alone is alter systems, shift norms, or absorb resistance at scale. Collective action changes what is possible not by replacing individual effort, but by extending it.

When people act together, effort compounds. Collective action allows responsibility to be distributed. Tasks are shared. Absences are absorbed. Momentum persists even when individual capacity fluctuates. This distribution is not merely practical. It is protective. It reduces burnout and increases resilience.

Scale also changes visibility. Individual actions may be effective without being widely seen. Collective action makes patterns harder to ignore. Repetition across people and contexts signals that an issue is not isolated. It draws attention not through volume alone, but through consistency.

Coordination further alters impact. When efforts align—even loosely—they reinforce one another. Duplication is reduced. Learning travels faster. Mistakes are corrected collectively rather than privately. Over time, coordinated action shapes expectations about what is normal, acceptable, or inevitable.

Importantly, collective action does not require uniformity. People participate for different reasons and at different levels of intensity. What matters is not consensus of belief, but overlap of behavior. Shared purpose can exist alongside disagreement, provided commitment is sustained.

Collective action also changes how resistance is encountered. Opposition that overwhelms individuals can be absorbed by groups. Pressure is shared. Risk is diffused without being erased. Persistence becomes possible where solitary effort would stall.

None of this diminishes the value of individual advocacy. It builds on it. Collective action is not a substitute for personal responsibility. It is what allows personal responsibility to scale without collapsing under its own weight.

The next section examines how collective action actually forms—without assuming movements, leaders, or centralized control.

Section 2

How Collective Action Actually Forms

Collective action rarely begins with organization. It begins with overlap. People act in proximity to one another, often without coordination, responding to similar conditions in similar ways. Over time, these parallel efforts intersect. Recognition follows. What was solitary becomes shared.

This is the earliest stage of collective action. Trust develops through observation. When people see others showing up consistently, uncertainty decreases. Reliability becomes visible. Participation feels less risky because effort is already underway and expectations are clearer.

From there, informal coordination emerges. Roles are not assigned at first. They are discovered. One person maintains continuity. Another communicates. Someone else brings resources or skills. Differentiation occurs naturally as people respond to what is needed rather than what is prescribed.

This kind of formation is adaptive. Because it is not tightly structured, it can adjust quickly. When circumstances change, roles shift. When participation fluctuates, effort redistributes. Collective action remains flexible rather than brittle.

Importantly, leadership at this stage is functional, not positional. Those who take initiative do so by addressing gaps, not by claiming authority. Influence follows contribution. Direction emerges from practice rather than declaration.

As coordination increases, shared language develops. People begin to articulate what they are doing and why. This articulation does not create the work; it reflects it. Purpose becomes clearer because action has already revealed what matters.

Collective action strengthens when communication supports coordination without imposing uniformity. Alignment is achieved through shared reference points rather than rigid agreement.

This process is gradual. It depends on time, visibility, and consistency. Attempts to force formation prematurely—through rigid plans or imposed structure—often disrupt these early dynamics. Collective action grows best when structure follows practice, not the other way around.

The next section examines how planning can support collective effort without creating false expectations or brittle designs.

Section 3

Planning Without Illusions

Planning is often mistaken for prediction. In collective action, plans rarely unfold as expected. Conditions shift. Participation fluctuates. External pressures intervene. Treating a plan as a fixed roadmap creates fragility. When reality diverges—as it inevitably does—momentum stalls.

Effective planning serves a different purpose. Rather than attempting to control outcomes, planning helps groups orient themselves. It clarifies near-term priorities, defines roles loosely, and establishes reference points that can be adjusted as circumstances change. A plan is not a promise. It is a working hypothesis.

This distinction matters. Plans that assume stability tend to overreach. They rely on sustained participation, consistent resources, and predictable responses. When those assumptions fail, disappointment follows. Planning without illusions accepts uncertainty from the outset.

Short horizons are protective. Focusing on what can be done next—rather than what must be achieved eventually—keeps effort grounded. It allows groups to learn from action, revise expectations, and adapt without losing direction. Progress is evaluated in steps, not declarations.

Planning also benefits from restraint. Not every possibility needs to be anticipated. Overplanning consumes energy that could be spent engaging. Simple structures—clear points of contact, agreed methods of communication, shared norms—often do more to sustain collective action than elaborate strategies.

Importantly, planning should remain provisional. As participation grows or contracts, plans must flex. Roles shift. Tactics change. What remains stable is not the plan itself, but the purpose it serves. When plans are treated as tools rather than commitments, adjustment feels like competence, not failure.

Planning without illusions does not avoid ambition. It tempers it with reality. By grounding effort in what is known, testable, and revisable, planning supports continuity without promising certainty.

The next section examines what happens when action encounters resistance—and how groups remain steady when progress is contested or slow.

Section 4

Action Meets Resistance

Resistance is not a sign that collective action has failed. It is often a sign that it has begun to matter. As efforts become more visible or effective, they encounter friction. This resistance can take many forms: skepticism, indifference, institutional delay, active opposition, or internal disagreement. None of these are unusual. They are part of the terrain.

Resistance operates externally and internally. External resistance appears when existing arrangements are challenged. Established interests may push back.

Processes slow. Rules are invoked selectively. Public narratives shift. These responses are rarely dramatic at first. More often, they are procedural, subtle, and persistent.

Internal resistance emerges as well. Within groups, differences in pace, priorities, and tolerance for risk surface over time. Fatigue accumulates. Frustration grows when progress is uneven or recognition is absent. Conflict does not necessarily reflect dysfunction. It often reflects commitment under strain.

How resistance is interpreted matters. When resistance is treated as a signal to escalate immediately, groups can overextend. When it is treated as proof that action is pointless, engagement collapses. Durable collective action takes a different approach. It treats resistance as information.

Resistance reveals where pressure is felt, where assumptions need revisiting, and where effort may require adjustment rather than intensification. It clarifies boundaries—what can be influenced directly, what requires patience, and what may need to be approached indirectly.

Steadiness is a strategic response. Maintaining consistent effort in the face of resistance often has more impact than reactive surges. Persistence normalizes participation. It reduces the effectiveness of obstruction by refusing to be derailed by delay or disagreement.

This does not mean ignoring safety or consequence. Some forms of resistance carry real risk. Groups must assess when exposure outweighs capacity and adjust accordingly. Protection of participants is part of sustainability, not a retreat from purpose.

Collective action is shaped as much by how it responds to resistance as by how it advances goals. Groups that endure are not those that avoid friction, but those that learn to move with it.

The next section looks to history—not for inspiration, but for patterns—examining what past efforts reveal about how collective action actually unfolds over time.

Section 5

What History Actually Shows

History is often invoked to motivate action. It is more useful when it is used to calibrate expectations. Popular accounts of collective action tend to compress timelines and elevate moments of visible change. Movements appear decisive. Progress looks linear. Leadership seems singular. This framing obscures the slower, uneven reality through which most collective efforts unfold.

Historical change is rarely driven by sudden consensus. More often, it emerges through prolonged periods of overlap, disagreement, and partial progress. Gains are incremental. Setbacks are common. Advances coexist with reversals. What persists is not unanimity, but continuity.

Many well-known movements relied less on constant mobilization than on sustained presence. Quiet work—maintaining institutions, protecting access, building relationships, preserving norms—often mattered as much as public confrontation. These efforts rarely drew attention, but they created conditions in which larger shifts became possible.

Leadership, in historical context, is also more distributed than commonly portrayed. While individual figures are remembered, most movements depended on networks of contributors who carried responsibility in different ways and at different times. Leadership rotated. Influence flowed through practice rather than title. Progress survived because responsibility was shared.

History also shows that conflict within movements is not an anomaly. Disagreement over strategy, pace, and priorities appears consistently across collective efforts. These tensions did not necessarily weaken movements. In many cases, they clarified direction and forced adaptation. The absence of conflict is not a sign of health. The inability to manage it is.

Perhaps most importantly, history reveals that endurance matters more than moments. Change that lasts is rarely achieved by peak intensity alone. It depends on the ability to remain engaged across long stretches where outcomes are unclear and recognition is minimal. The work continues between milestones.

This perspective does not diminish the significance of collective action. It grounds it. When expectations are aligned with historical reality, disappointment loses some of its power. Groups are better prepared to adjust, persist, and renew effort rather than abandoning it when progress slows.

The final section reframes collective action as a long-term practice—one that depends less on momentum than on continuity.

Section 6

Collective Action as a Long Game

Collective action is often judged by moments of visibility. Its real measure is continuity. Efforts that endure do so not because they remain intense, but because they are renewed. Participation ebbs and flows. Roles change. Circumstances shift. What allows collective action to persist is the ability to absorb these changes without losing direction.

This is what makes collective action a long game. Rather than relying on constant mobilization, durable efforts build infrastructure—formal or informal—that supports participation over time. Shared norms, routines, communication channels, and role flexibility allow engagement to continue even as individual involvement fluctuates.

Renewal is central to this process. People step forward and step back. New participants join. Others leave. Collective action remains viable when these transitions are expected rather than treated as failures. Continuity is maintained through succession, adaptation, and shared ownership of purpose.

Collective action also benefits from memory. Experiences accumulate. Lessons are retained. Mistakes inform future decisions. When knowledge is held collectively rather than individually, progress does not reset each time participation changes. The group learns, even as its composition shifts.

Importantly, a long-game approach resists urgency as a default mode. Urgency has its place, particularly in moments of acute threat. But when urgency becomes constant, it erodes judgment and exhausts capacity. Collective action that treats urgency as occasional rather than permanent preserves attention and discernment.

This perspective changes how success is understood. Success is not only measured by outcomes achieved, but by capacity sustained. The ability to remain engaged, to recover from setbacks, and to continue adjusting over time is itself a form of progress.

Collective action does not culminate. It evolves. When effort is framed as an ongoing practice rather than a campaign, participation becomes less fragile. Responsibility is shared. Renewal is possible. The work continues without requiring constant escalation.

The next chapter turns to the systems that mediate engagement—beginning with the information environment that shapes how collective effort is perceived, directed, and sustained.

CHAPTER 6

Staying Oriented in an Information-Rich Environment

Section 1

Why Being Informed Is a Form of Responsibility

In an information-rich environment, being informed is not a neutral state. What people attend to, believe, and repeat shapes the conditions under which decisions are made. Information influences perception. Perception guides action. In this sense, how individuals relate to information carries consequence beyond personal preference.

Responsibility enters at this point. Being informed does not mean consuming more content. It means engaging with information in a way that supports judgment rather than reaction. The difference matters. Exposure alone does not improve understanding. In many cases, it does the opposite.

Modern information systems are designed to maximize attention, not clarity. Content that provokes fear, outrage, or certainty travels faster than content that encourages reflection. Over time, this skews perception. Issues appear more polarized, more urgent, and more irresolvable than they often are.

When perception distorts, participation follows. People withdraw because everything feels unstable. Or they react quickly, aligning with positions that promise clarity without requiring examination. Neither response supports sustained engagement. Both erode trust—in institutions, in others, and eventually in one's own judgment.

Being informed, in this context, requires restraint. It involves selecting sources carefully, tolerating uncertainty, and resisting the pressure to respond immediately. It also involves recognizing when information is incomplete, misleading, or framed to provoke rather than explain.

This is not a call for detachment. Information matters because it shapes what people believe is possible. When information is handled carelessly, it narrows imagination and hardens positions. When it is handled with care, it supports discernment and proportion.

Responsibility here is not about expertise. It is about orientation. Staying oriented means maintaining a workable sense of what is happening, what is known, and what remains uncertain—without becoming overwhelmed or reactive. It allows engagement to remain grounded even when information is noisy or contested.

The sections that follow examine how information distorts participation, how critical thinking functions as an ongoing practice, and how people remain informed without becoming cynical or consumed.

Section 2

How Information Distorts Participation

Information does not only inform. It shapes how participation feels. When information environments emphasize speed, volume, and reaction, they alter the conditions under which people decide whether to engage at all. Distortion enters not through falsehood alone, but through imbalance—what is amplified, what is omitted, and how attention is guided.

One common distortion is compression. Complex issues are reduced to simplified frames that favor certainty over accuracy. Nuance is lost. Context is stripped away. Positions harden because they are presented as complete rather than provisional. When problems are flattened in this way, meaningful engagement becomes difficult. People either align quickly or disengage entirely.

Another distortion is amplification. Content that provokes fear, outrage, or tribal loyalty is rewarded with visibility. This creates a feedback loop in which extreme or emotionally charged perspectives dominate perception, even when they represent a minority view. The result is a public landscape that appears more polarized and volatile than lived reality often is.

This amplification skews expectations. People begin to assume that disagreement is hostility and that participation will invite conflict. For some, this leads to withdrawal. For others, it encourages performative alignment—taking positions that signal belonging rather than contribute understanding.

A third distortion is fragmentation. Information arrives disconnected from broader narratives. Headlines appear without follow-up. Events are encountered without continuity. Attention moves on before understanding can settle. Participation becomes reactive, responding to isolated moments rather than sustained conditions.

Fragmentation undermines patience. When issues appear as a stream of crises rather than ongoing challenges, people struggle to maintain proportion. Urgency crowds out judgment. Long-term engagement feels impossible because nothing appears stable long enough to work on.

Finally, there is distortion through saturation. Constant exposure to information—particularly distressing or conflicting information—erodes capacity. Mental bandwidth contracts. Decision fatigue sets in. Under these conditions, opting out begins to feel like self-preservation.

None of these distortions require misinformation to operate. They arise from structure, not intent. Understanding this matters because it shifts responsibility away from individual virtue and toward environmental awareness. People do not disengage because they lack concern. They disengage because the information environment makes sustained attention difficult to maintain.

Recognizing distortion allows for adjustment. When people become aware of how information shapes perception, they regain some agency over how they engage. They can slow intake, seek context, and resist immediate alignment. Participation becomes more deliberate and less reactive.

The next section examines critical thinking as an ongoing practice—not as a posture or identity, but as a way of regulating attention and judgment within a distorted information environment.

Section 3

Critical Thinking as Ongoing Practice

Critical thinking is often treated as a stance—something one claims rather than something one does. In practice, critical thinking functions less as a position and more as a process. It is not about perpetual doubt or contrarianism. It is about regulating attention, judgment, and response in environments that reward speed and certainty.

As an ongoing practice, critical thinking begins with pacing. Rather than reacting immediately to new information, it creates space for assessment. This pause allows questions to surface: What is the source? What is missing? How does this fit with what is already known? Slowing down is not avoidance. It is a condition for discernment.

Context is central to this practice. Information rarely stands on its own. Understanding requires placing facts within broader patterns, histories, and constraints. Without context, even accurate information can mislead. Critical thinking restores proportion by reconnecting details to their larger frame.

Another element is tolerance for uncertainty. Many issues do not resolve cleanly. Evidence may be incomplete. Perspectives may conflict. Critical thinking resists the urge to force closure where it does not yet exist. This tolerance prevents premature alignment and keeps engagement flexible.

Critical thinking also involves examining one's own responses. Emotional reactions are not obstacles to thinking, but signals. They indicate where values are engaged and where perception may be narrowing. Recognizing these responses allows individuals to distinguish between information that informs and information that provokes.

Importantly, critical thinking is not synonymous with cynicism. Skepticism that hardens into dismissal undermines engagement as much as uncritical acceptance.

Critical thinking occupies a middle ground—open to information, but not governed by it.

Because information environments change, this practice never ends. New platforms emerge. Incentives shift. Narratives evolve. Critical thinking remains effective only when it adapts, remaining attentive to how information is framed and delivered.

As a practice, critical thinking supports sustained participation by preserving judgment under pressure. It allows people to stay engaged without becoming reactive, rigid, or disengaged.

The next section examines how verification can be approached without sliding into cynicism or paralysis—maintaining care without exhausting trust.

Section 4

Verifying Without Becoming Cynical

Verification is often framed as distrust. In practice, it is a form of care—care for accuracy, for consequence, and for the impact information has on judgment and action. Verification becomes corrosive only when it hardens into cynicism, where nothing is trusted and engagement stalls.

The difference lies in posture. Cynicism assumes bad faith as a default. Verification assumes fallibility. These are not the same. Most distortions in information environments arise not from deliberate deception, but from incentives that reward speed, visibility, and certainty. Verification responds to these conditions without retreating from engagement.

Effective verification is selective. Not every claim requires the same level of scrutiny. People conserve attention by focusing verification where stakes are higher or uncertainty is greater. This prioritization prevents exhaustion and allows discernment to be applied where it matters most.

Verification also benefits from triangulation. Relying on a single source—regardless of its perceived credibility—creates vulnerability. Cross-referencing perspectives, methods, and data points restores balance. Agreement across independent sources does not guarantee truth, but it increases confidence that information is not narrowly framed.

Importantly, verification does not require complete certainty. Waiting for absolute confirmation before forming judgment often results in paralysis. Responsible verification aims for sufficiency rather than perfection—enough clarity to act proportionally, with openness to revision as new information emerges.

This approach protects trust. When people treat verification as an ongoing process rather than a final verdict, trust remains conditional rather than absent. Institutions, sources, and individuals are evaluated based on patterns over time, not isolated claims.

Verification also includes recognizing limits. Some information cannot be easily confirmed. Some processes remain opaque. Acknowledging these limits prevents overconfidence and reduces the temptation to fill gaps with speculation.

Verifying without becoming cynical allows engagement to continue under uncertainty. It preserves the ability to act without requiring absolute assurance and to adjust without losing credibility.

The final section examines how people stay informed without becoming consumed—how boundaries around attention protect engagement in an information-saturated environment.

Section 5

Staying Informed Without Being Consumed

Staying informed is necessary. Being consumed by information is not. When attention is continuously captured by updates, commentary, and competing narratives, capacity erodes. Judgment narrows. Engagement becomes reactive or avoidant. The goal of information stewardship is not maximal awareness, but workable orientation.

Boundaries matter. People remain engaged longer when they regulate how, when, and why they take in information. This includes limiting exposure to cycles of breaking news, choosing sources deliberately, and allowing periods where attention is directed elsewhere. These boundaries are not disengagement. They are maintenance.

Information intake should serve understanding, not replace it. When consumption outpaces integration, meaning does not accumulate. Facts blur together. Context dissolves. Pausing to reflect—individually or with others—allows information to settle into patterns that support judgment.

Staying informed also requires acceptance of incompleteness. No one has access to all relevant information. Attempts to achieve total awareness often lead to fatigue or false certainty. Sustainable engagement accepts partial knowledge and works within it, revising understanding as conditions change.

Social reinforcement plays a role here. Conversations that prioritize curiosity over performance support orientation. Spaces that allow questions, uncertainty, and disagreement without escalation make it easier to remain informed without becoming rigid or defensive.

Most importantly, information should remain connected to purpose. When information intake is detached from action or reflection, it becomes noise. When it is connected to what people are actually trying to understand, protect, or improve, it retains relevance without overwhelming attention.

Staying informed without being consumed allows engagement to persist. It preserves capacity. It supports proportion. It keeps participation grounded rather than reactive.

With this orientation in place, the next chapter turns to how collective efforts process difference—examining how inclusion, power, and perspective shape judgment before engagement ever reaches formal institutions.

CHAPTER 7

Difference, Inclusion, and Collective Intelligence

Section 1

Why Difference Improves Collective Judgment

Groups make better decisions when they see more of the problem. Homogeneous perspectives tend to converge quickly. Agreement comes easily. Confidence builds early. But early agreement often reflects shared assumptions rather than accurate understanding. What looks like cohesion can conceal missing information.

Difference interrupts that process. When people bring varied experiences, constraints, and priorities into a shared effort, assumptions are more likely to surface. Questions are asked that would otherwise go unspoken. Risks become visible sooner. The problem itself is defined more accurately before solutions are proposed.

This matters because many failures in collective action occur upstream. Effort is applied to the wrong leverage point. Resources are directed toward symptoms rather than causes. Strategies are chosen that work well for some participants while imposing hidden costs on others. These missteps often trace back to incomplete perspective rather than lack of commitment.

Difference improves judgment by widening the frame. People who experience consequences differently notice different pressures. Those who operate closer to impact see details that planners miss. Those with less margin for error often recognize risk sooner. When these perspectives are absent, groups underestimate friction and overestimate feasibility.

This is not an argument for unanimity or balance for its own sake. Difference does not guarantee better outcomes. It introduces tension. It slows consensus. It complicates coordination. But those costs are often smaller than the cost of proceeding confidently with an incomplete view.

Collective intelligence emerges when disagreement is informative rather than obstructive. That requires conditions where difference can surface without being dismissed, delayed, or absorbed into the dominant frame. It requires attention to how decisions are formed—not just who is present, but whose perspective shapes conclusions.

The sections that follow examine how inclusion functions structurally, how listening operates as discipline rather than virtue, and how power and perspective influence what collective efforts are able to see.

Section 2

Inclusion as Structure, Not Sentiment

Inclusion is often framed as attitude. It is discussed in terms of openness, goodwill, or intention. While these qualities may influence behavior, they do not determine outcomes on their own. Inclusion that depends on personal disposition is fragile. It fluctuates with mood, pressure, and context.

Sustained inclusion is structural. It is shaped by how decisions are made, how information flows, and how participation is enabled or constrained. Structure determines whose perspectives are present at critical moments and whose are filtered out before they can influence judgment.

This distinction matters. Groups can value inclusion in principle while reproducing exclusion in practice. Meetings are held at inaccessible times. Input is gathered but not integrated. Participation is welcomed but carries unspoken costs. None of this requires ill intent. It emerges from design choices left unexamined.

Structural inclusion begins with access. Who is able to participate consistently? Who has the time, resources, and safety to contribute without penalty? When access is uneven, perspectives disappear—not because they lack relevance, but because participation carries disproportionate burden.

Inclusion also depends on process. How are decisions formed? Who frames the questions? At what point are alternatives considered closed? When processes privilege speed, familiarity, or consensus, difference is often sidelined before it can do its work.

Feedback mechanisms play a role as well. When people do not see how their input affects outcomes, participation erodes. Inclusion becomes symbolic rather than functional. Durable inclusion requires visible pathways between contribution and consequence.

Importantly, structure does not eliminate discretion. Design sets conditions. People still make choices within them. But when structures support inclusion, individual effort is amplified rather than isolated. Responsibility for inclusion shifts from personal virtue to collective practice.

Inclusion, understood this way, is not about making everyone comfortable. It is about ensuring that relevant perspectives can surface, be heard, and shape decisions—even when doing so introduces tension or delay.

The next section examines listening as a discipline: how attention is sustained in the presence of difference, and how groups avoid confusing hearing with understanding.

Section 3

Listening as a Discipline

Listening is often treated as a courtesy. In collective work, it functions as a discipline. Courtesy depends on intent. Discipline depends on practice. When listening is left to disposition alone, it degrades under pressure. Time constraints, disagreement, and hierarchy all narrow attention. What remains is hearing without understanding.

Disciplined listening is different. It requires sustained attention to perspectives that complicate one's own. This includes not only what is said, but what is emphasized, avoided, or constrained by circumstance. Listening at this level is effortful. It demands restraint—particularly the restraint to postpone response.

In groups, listening is shaped by structure as much as skill. Who speaks first, who summarizes, and who frames conclusions all influence what is heard. When dominant perspectives set the terms early, alternative views are often filtered through them rather than considered on their own terms. Disciplined listening requires interrupting this pattern.

This does not mean equal airtime. Listening as a discipline prioritizes relevance over symmetry. Some perspectives carry information others do not. The task is not to balance voices abstractly, but to ensure that decision-relevant experience is not overridden by familiarity or authority.

Listening also requires tolerance for discomfort. Difference introduces friction. It slows agreement. It surfaces conflict. Groups that equate harmony with effectiveness often suppress this friction prematurely. Disciplined listening allows tension to persist long enough for its informational value to be realized.

Importantly, listening does not require agreement. Understanding another perspective does not obligate endorsement. Conflating the two shuts down inquiry. When listening is treated as a commitment to consensus, people protect themselves by withholding perspective altogether.

Listening as a discipline creates conditions for learning. When attention is sustained, assumptions can be examined. Blind spots emerge. Judgment improves. Over time, groups become better at distinguishing disagreement that informs from disagreement that obstructs.

The next section examines how power and privilege shape whose perspectives are easier to hear—and how awareness of those dynamics sharpens, rather than weakens, collective intelligence.

Section 4

Power, Privilege, and Perspective

Power shapes what is visible. In any collective setting, some perspectives travel more easily than others. They are heard sooner, trusted faster, and treated as representative. This is not always the result of intention. It often reflects how power and privilege operate quietly within systems.

Privilege influences perspective by reducing friction. Those with greater access, security, or authority encounter fewer barriers when participating. Their experiences are less constrained by risk or consequence. As a result, their interpretations often feel neutral or universal, even when they are not.

This has implications for collective judgment. Perspectives formed under conditions of relative safety may underestimate cost, delay, or unintended impact. Conversely, perspectives shaped by constraint often detect risk earlier and more precisely. When these differences are ignored, decisions skew toward feasibility on paper rather than viability in practice.

Recognizing power does not mean discounting contribution. Awareness of privilege is not a demand for silence. It is a call for calibration. It invites those with greater influence to listen longer, question assumptions more carefully, and resist the impulse to generalize from limited experience.

Similarly, acknowledging power does not assign authority automatically to those with less of it. Perspective is shaped by position, not purified by it. The goal is not to invert hierarchy, but to surface information that would otherwise remain hidden.

Power becomes problematic when it is invisible. When influence is unexamined, dominant perspectives define what counts as reasonable, urgent, or realistic. Alternatives appear marginal not because they lack merit, but because they challenge established frames. Collective intelligence declines when these dynamics go unaddressed.

Structural awareness sharpens judgment. When groups account for how power and privilege shape participation, they gain a more accurate map of the problem space. Decisions are informed by a fuller range of experience. Risks are identified earlier. Trade-offs are understood more clearly.

This awareness does not weaken collective effort. It strengthens it. The next section examines how groups learn without performance—how difference is integrated over time without turning inclusion into display or debate into theater.

Section 5

Learning Without Performance

Learning in collective settings is often made visible. People signal openness. They announce growth. They demonstrate awareness. While visibility can reinforce norms, it can also distort learning when performance replaces integration.

Learning that is performed tends to stay shallow. When attention is focused on signaling correctness or alignment, curiosity narrows. Questions become risky. Uncertainty is hidden. The goal shifts from understanding to appearing informed. Over time, this undermines judgment rather than improving it.

Durable learning is quieter. It shows up in changed decisions, revised assumptions, and adjusted behavior. It does not require constant articulation. In fact, some of the most consequential learning occurs without immediate acknowledgment, as perspectives are absorbed and applied over time.

This distinction matters in groups. When learning is treated as a public test, participation contracts. People with less social capital, less fluency, or higher risk hesitate to contribute. Difference is filtered before it can inform. Collective intelligence declines under the pressure to perform.

Learning without performance requires tolerance for process. Understanding develops unevenly. People revisit ideas. Mistakes recur. Insight arrives gradually. Groups that allow this process to unfold without forcing display retain more participants and extract more value from difference.

It also requires separating accountability from spectacle. Groups still need to address harm, correct error, and revise behavior. But when correction becomes performative, learning stalls. Responsibility is best sustained when it is specific, proportionate, and oriented toward future action rather than public demonstration.

Learning, in this sense, is cumulative. It builds through repeated exposure, reflection, and adjustment. Over time, shared understanding deepens—not because everyone agrees, but because the group has learned how to learn together.

The final section considers difference as a long-term asset—how sustained inclusion strengthens collective intelligence across time rather than merely improving individual moments of decision.

Section 6

Difference as a Long-Term Asset

Difference is often treated as a challenge to be managed. Over time, it functions as an asset to be maintained. When groups engage difference only episodically—during moments of crisis or controversy—its value is limited. Perspectives surface briefly, tensions rise, and attention shifts elsewhere. The learning does not accumulate. Collective intelligence remains shallow.

Difference becomes an asset when it is sustained. This requires structures that keep varied perspectives present across time, not just at moments of decision. It also requires norms that allow disagreement to inform judgment without destabilizing participation. Over time, these conditions compound.

Groups that maintain difference learn faster. They detect risk earlier. They adapt more readily to change. They are less surprised by consequences that fall unevenly across participants. Because assumptions are regularly tested, strategies remain grounded in lived conditions rather than abstract models.

Difference also protects against stagnation. Homogeneous groups tend to reinforce existing frames. Innovation slows. Blind spots widen. Sustained difference interrupts this drift by continually reintroducing constraint, context, and alternative interpretation. It keeps judgment elastic rather than brittle.

Importantly, difference does not eliminate the need for coordination. Collective intelligence depends on integration as well as diversity. The goal is not perpetual disagreement, but informed convergence—decisions shaped by a wider range of experience and refined through disciplined listening and structural inclusion.

Over time, this integration becomes a capability. Groups that have learned to work with difference do not need to relearn it each time conditions change. They carry the capacity forward. New members adapt more quickly. Transitions are less disruptive. Judgment improves not because individuals are exceptional, but because the system is designed to learn.

Difference, sustained in this way, strengthens collective effort. It does not guarantee success. It improves the quality of choice.

The next chapter examines what happens when collective intelligence breaks down—how division, conflict, and fear erode capacity, and what forms of repair make continued engagement possible before formal institutions can play any role.

CHAPTER 8
Division, Conflict, and the Work of Repair

DIVISION, CONFLICT, AND THE WORK OF REPAIR

Section 1

How Division Undermines Collective Capacity

Division weakens collective effort before it hardens positions. Long before disagreement becomes overt conflict, capacity erodes. Attention narrows. Trust thins. Coordination becomes costly. People spend more energy managing friction than addressing shared problems.

This is the practical consequence of division. When groups fracture, information no longer moves freely. Signals are filtered through identity and alignment. Warnings from outside one's own circle are discounted. Learning slows because correction is interpreted as threat rather than feedback.

Division also alters how risk is perceived. Actions taken by others are read through suspicion. Intent is inferred negatively. Ambiguity is resolved against trust. Under these conditions, even neutral behavior can escalate tension. Effort shifts from problem-solving to position-protecting.

Capacity loss compounds over time. As coordination becomes more difficult, participation declines. People disengage not because they lack concern, but because the cost of engagement rises. Meetings feel unproductive. Collaboration feels fragile. Withdrawal appears rational.

Importantly, division does not require hatred to operate. It can arise from difference combined with fear, from misaligned incentives, or from environments that reward outrage and certainty. Once present, it becomes self-reinforcing. Reduced contact confirms assumptions. Assumptions justify further separation.

This dynamic undermines collective intelligence. Groups lose access to corrective perspective. Blind spots widen. Decisions are made with incomplete information and increased confidence. Errors persist longer because admitting them feels like concession rather than adjustment. Repair becomes harder as division deepens, not because people become worse, but because the conditions supporting cooperation deteriorate.

Understanding division as a capacity problem changes the response. It shifts attention from persuading individuals to repairing environments. The question becomes not "Who is wrong?" but "What conditions are preventing coordination, learning, and shared effort?"

The sections that follow examine how fear and identity intensify opposition, what repair can realistically accomplish, and what conditions allow engagement to persist even when agreement is limited.

Section 2

Fear, Identity, and the Logic of Opposition

Opposition often appears ideological. At a deeper level, it is frequently adaptive. When people feel threatened—economically, culturally, or socially—they seek stability. Identity provides that stability. It offers belonging, predictability, and a framework for interpreting uncertainty. Under these conditions, opposition becomes a way of protecting coherence rather than rejecting cooperation.

Fear sharpens boundaries. Ambiguous information is interpreted defensively. Difference is perceived as risk. Nuance collapses because it requires tolerance for uncertainty. What remains are simplified categories that distinguish "us" from "them."

Identity intensifies this process. When beliefs become tied to group membership, disagreement feels personal. Challenges to ideas are experienced as challenges to belonging. In response, positions harden. Flexibility decreases not because evidence is absent, but because changing one's mind carries a social cost.

This dynamic follows a recognizable logic. Under perceived threat, people prioritize loyalty over accuracy. They seek confirmation rather than correction.

Signals from within the group are trusted more readily than signals from outside it, regardless of content. Opposition becomes self-reinforcing as shared narratives solidify.

Importantly, this does not require misinformation. Even accurate information can be rejected if it arrives from an untrusted source or threatens identity stability. The issue is not truth versus falsehood, but safety versus uncertainty.

Understanding this logic matters for repair. Attempts to confront opposition solely with facts often fail because they ignore the conditions driving resistance. When fear is present, information that increases uncertainty feels dangerous rather than helpful.

Repair efforts that overlook identity dynamics risk escalation. Pressure to concede, explain, or justify can deepen opposition by increasing perceived threat. People retreat further into group narratives where coherence is preserved and challenge is contained.

Recognizing the role of fear and identity does not excuse harm or entrenchment. It clarifies the terrain. Effective repair works by reducing threat, widening perceived safety, and creating conditions where uncertainty becomes tolerable again. Only then can difference re-enter the space as information rather than danger.

The next section examines what repair can and cannot realistically accomplish—setting boundaries that prevent false expectations and symbolic gestures from undermining sustained engagement.

Section 3

What Repair Can and Cannot Do

Repair is often misunderstood as reconciliation. People expect it to restore harmony, resolve disagreement, or return relationships to a prior state. These expectations set repair up to fail. In deeply divided contexts, repair rarely produces consensus or closure. What it can do is restore enough capacity for shared work to resume.

Repair operates within limits. It cannot erase difference. It cannot guarantee trust. It cannot force openness where fear remains high. Attempts to promise these outcomes often undermine credibility and increase frustration when results fall short.

What repair can do is stabilize conditions. It can reduce escalation. It can reopen channels of communication. It can make coordination possible where it had broken down. These outcomes may appear modest, but they are foundational. Without them, collective effort stalls regardless of intent.

Repair also clarifies boundaries. Not every relationship can be mended. Not every conflict can be bridged. Some positions are incompatible in practice. Recognizing this prevents repair work from becoming coercive or performative. Repair loses integrity when it demands participation or equates refusal with failure.

Importantly, repair is not neutral. Decisions about what to repair, when to engage, and where to invest effort reflect values and priorities. Repair work involves judgment about feasibility, risk, and proportion. Treating it as purely technical obscures these choices and invites misunderstanding.

Repair is also not symmetrical. Harms are experienced unevenly. Power is distributed unequally. Expecting all parties to contribute equally to repair ignores these realities and can reproduce the very dynamics repair seeks to address. Effective repair accounts for asymmetry rather than pretending it does not exist.

What repair can reliably offer is containment. By setting expectations appropriately, repair efforts can prevent further deterioration even when deeper change is slow. They create space where learning can resume and where disagreement does not immediately collapse into withdrawal or hostility. Repair, understood this way, is not a solution. It is a condition.

The next section examines the conditions that make repair possible in practice—

focusing on design choices that reduce threat, support patience, and allow engagement to persist without illusion.

Section 4

Conditions That Make Repair Possible

Repair does not begin with agreement. It begins with conditions that make engagement tolerable again. When division is driven by fear and identity threat, repair efforts fail if they increase exposure or demand premature vulnerability. What makes repair possible is not dialogue alone, but environments that reduce perceived risk and allow uncertainty to be held without escalation.

Safety is foundational. People are more willing to re-engage when participation does not carry immediate social, professional, or emotional penalty. This includes protection from ridicule, retaliation, or forced disclosure. Safety does not mean comfort. It means that disagreement does not automatically trigger punishment or exclusion.

Time is another condition. Repair unfolds slowly. Trust, when it returns, does so incrementally. Attempts to accelerate this process often backfire by signaling impatience or hidden agendas. Allowing time for contact, repetition, and adjustment gives fear space to subside and curiosity to reemerge.

Structure matters as much as intent. Clear norms around participation—how decisions are made, how conflict is addressed, and how consequences are handled—reduce ambiguity. When expectations are predictable, people expend less energy on self-protection and more on understanding.

Third-party facilitation can support repair. When tensions are high, neutral structures or facilitators can hold boundaries that participants cannot hold alone. This does not remove responsibility from those involved. It redistributes it in ways that reduce escalation and preserve capacity.

Importantly, repair benefits from limited scope. Small, specific goals are more effective than broad appeals to unity. Repair is strengthened when it is anchored to concrete tasks or shared responsibilities rather than abstract reconciliation. Working together on bounded problems rebuilds coordination before attempting deeper alignment.

Finally, repair requires patience without passivity. Reducing threat does not mean avoiding conflict indefinitely. It means sequencing engagement so that learning is possible. Pressure applied too early hardens resistance. Pressure applied too late allows drift. Effective repair adjusts pace in response to capacity. These conditions do not guarantee resolution. They make continued engagement possible.

The final section reframes repair as ongoing maintenance—how engagement is sustained without false expectations or the promise of closure.

Section 5

Sustaining Engagement Without Illusion

Repair is rarely complete. In divided environments, expecting closure or lasting harmony creates disappointment and withdrawal. Engagement weakens when people believe that effort should eventually eliminate tension altogether. In reality, difference and conflict remain features of collective life.

Sustaining engagement requires accepting this. Rather than aiming for resolution, durable efforts focus on manageability. The goal is not to erase disagreement, but to prevent it from overwhelming capacity. Engagement persists when conflict can be contained, navigated, and revisited without collapsing cooperation.

This perspective changes how success is measured. Progress is not defined by consensus reached or relationships restored. It is defined by participation sustained, coordination maintained, and learning preserved over time. These outcomes may appear modest, but they are essential.

Illusions are costly. Promises of unity, healing, or permanent repair raise expectations that cannot be met. When those expectations fail, cynicism grows. People disengage not because repair was ineffective, but because it was misrepresented.

Honest framing protects effort. When participants understand that repair is ongoing and incomplete by nature, setbacks feel less like betrayal and more like part of the work. Adjustments are expected. Persistence becomes possible.

Sustained engagement also depends on boundaries. Not all conflicts are immediately workable. Not all relationships can be repaired at the same pace. Recognizing limits allows effort to be directed where it can have effect, without exhausting capacity on situations that are not yet tractable.

Repair, in this sense, is maintenance. It involves repeated attention to conditions, norms, and structures that allow participation to continue despite disagreement. Like other forms of maintenance, it is rarely dramatic. Its value lies in what it prevents: escalation, fragmentation, and withdrawal.

Engagement endures when expectations remain grounded. Repair does not deliver harmony. It preserves the possibility of working together.

With this understanding, the next chapter turns to institutions—examining how formal structures can either support this ongoing work or undermine it through rigidity, misalignment, or neglect.

WHEN ENGAGEMENT PRODUCES MORE THAN INTENDED

CHAPTER 9

When Engagement Produces More Than Intended

WHEN ENGAGEMENT PRODUCES MORE THAN INTENDED

Section 1

What These Cases Have in Common

Engagement does not always produce the outcomes people set out to achieve. Often, its most durable effects emerge indirectly—through changes in routine, relationship, or expectation that were not part of the original intent. These secondary effects are easy to miss because they do not announce themselves as successes. They accumulate quietly, shaping conditions rather than delivering conclusions.

The cases that follow share this pattern. In each, individuals or small groups acted in response to immediate, local conditions. Their efforts were modest in scope and practical in orientation. None began with an explicit aim to influence institutions or produce systemic change. They were focused on maintaining something that mattered within reach.

Yet over time, those actions altered more than the immediate situation. New relationships formed. Informal coordination took shape. Expectations shifted about what was possible, acceptable, or worth addressing. In some cases, institutions responded—not because they were pressured directly, but because conditions had changed around them.

This is not accidental. Engagement that is sustained and visible creates signals. It demonstrates viability. It reduces uncertainty. It reveals gaps between how systems operate and how people actually live. These signals travel outward, often reaching actors who were not part of the original effort.

What matters here is not scale, but continuity. The actions described did not grow rapidly or dramatically. They persisted. That persistence made them legible to others. Over time, what began as maintenance became reference. What began as response became expectation.

These cases also share restraint. No single actor attempted to control outcomes beyond their capacity. Effort remained proportionate. Boundaries were respected.

This restraint allowed engagement to continue long enough for secondary effects to emerge.

The sections that follow present three such cases. They are not models to be replicated or lessons to be extracted mechanically. They are illustrations of how sustained engagement, grounded in ordinary life, can produce effects that exceed intention without exceeding capacity.

The final section returns to analysis, identifying what these cases reveal about how engagement interacts with systems and institutions over time.

Section 2

The Workday

The engagement began as part of a routine. A small group of neighbors shared responsibility for maintaining a modest community garden located along a daily walking route. The task was practical: watering, clearing debris, replacing plants that did not survive. There was no formal schedule and no stated goal beyond keeping the space usable.

Participation fit into the workday rather than displacing it. People stopped by before heading to work or on the way home. Time spent was measured in minutes, not hours. Responsibility rotated informally based on availability. No one coordinated the effort in advance; it persisted because it was easy to fold into existing patterns.

Over time, something else changed. Regular presence made the work visible. Others began to recognize the routine and adjust around it. Conversations formed briefly—about weather, plant choices, timing. These exchanges were incidental, but they accumulated. The space became predictable, and with predictability came a sense of shared ownership.

The work itself remained modest. What expanded was coordination. Tools were left in accessible places. Tasks were anticipated rather than discovered. Small problems were addressed before they escalated. None of this required instruction or leadership. It emerged through repetition.

The secondary effects were subtle. People who did not participate directly altered how they treated the space. Litter decreased. Damage was addressed more quickly. Use became more considerate. The garden did not become a symbol or a cause. It became part of the neighborhood's working environment.

Eventually, local staff responsible for public maintenance took notice. The change was not framed as a request or a campaign. It appeared as a condition that was already being maintained. Support followed in small ways—replacement soil, occasional repairs, coordination around utilities. The response was incremental and pragmatic.

Nothing about the effort scaled dramatically. What mattered was that routine engagement created legibility. The workday rhythm made the activity intelligible to others and durable over time. Secondary effects emerged not from intention, but from continuity.

The next case examines a different setting—one shaped less by routine and more by access—showing how sustained engagement can surface procedural gaps and invite institutional response without direct advocacy.

Section 3

The Access Issue

The issue surfaced through use rather than complaint. A public access point along a shoreline was technically open but increasingly difficult to use in practice. Parking was restricted. Signage was inconsistent or ambiguous. Pathways were obstructed or uneven. People adapted individually—arriving earlier, parking farther away, improvising routes—but the friction accumulated.

When Engagement Produces More Than Intended

Engagement began informally. Regular users started sharing information about access conditions: tides, temporary barriers, enforcement patterns, and workarounds. These exchanges were initially practical rather than political. The aim was not to contest authority, but to make continued use possible.

As coordination increased, patterns became visible. The same obstacles recurred. Certain users were disproportionately affected. Enforcement appeared inconsistent. What had seemed like isolated inconveniences resolved into a recognizable pattern of constrained access. This shift did not immediately produce outrage, but it did produce clarity—a shared understanding that the problem was not incidental.

That clarity changed the nature of engagement. Once the limits of informal adjustment became apparent, users began documenting conditions and raising questions publicly. Meetings were requested. Town officials were pressed to explain how access was defined, enforced, and maintained. What had started as adaptive coordination became structured confrontation—not personal, but institutional.

At this stage, the issue entered governance. Public meetings formalized what repeated use had already revealed: a gap between stated access rights and lived reality. Ambiguity that had once been navigable now demanded resolution. Administrators could no longer rely on informal discretion. The system was required to clarify itself.

The response extended beyond procedural fixes. While some adjustments were made—signage revised, maintenance schedules altered—it became clear that incremental changes could not resolve the underlying conflict. Access depended on definitions that were unclear, unevenly applied, or contested. Resolution ultimately required legislative action to establish enforceable boundaries and obligations.

The outcome was not the absence of confrontation, but its completion. A new law clarified access rights and responsibilities, reducing uncertainty for users, administrators, and property owners alike. The system did not adapt quietly; it adapted because sustained engagement made ambiguity untenable.

This case illustrates how engagement often unfolds in phases: beginning with use, moving through informal coordination, escalating into institutional confrontation, and concluding—when necessary—with formal policy change. Informal engagement did not fail; it reached its limit. Law became the mechanism by which visibility was converted into durable resolution.

The next case shifts again—from access to care—examining what happens when even formal engagement reaches its boundary, and institutions are slow or unable to respond.

Section 4

The After-School Gap

The gap appeared gradually. A small group of parents and caregivers noticed that after-school hours were becoming increasingly difficult to manage. School dismissal times did not align with work schedules. Formal programs were limited, expensive, or full. Families adapted privately, trading favors and adjusting routines where possible.

Coordination began out of necessity. Caregivers shared pickup responsibilities on an informal basis. Children moved between homes depending on availability. The arrangements were practical and provisional, changing week to week as schedules shifted. No one intended to create a program. The goal was to get through the afternoons safely.

Over time, the coordination stabilized. Patterns formed. Certain households became regular anchors. Communication improved. Expectations clarified. What began as ad hoc support turned into a dependable, if fragile, system of care.

The limits of this system eventually became clear. As participation increased, the burden concentrated. Liability concerns surfaced. Space constraints mattered. The informal network could absorb some fluctuation, but not growth. The effort had reached the edge of what private coordination could reasonably sustain.

This constraint produced visibility. Teachers, administrators, and local staff became aware of the arrangements through ordinary interaction. Children referenced routines. Schedules overlapped. The gap between institutional dismissal policies and lived realities became apparent without formal complaint.

Response followed condition, not pressure. Administrators explored modest extensions to existing programs. Partnerships with community organizations were considered. Pilot solutions were tested rather than announced. None of this was immediate or comprehensive, but the problem had become concrete enough to engage.

The informal effort did not disappear. It adjusted as institutional support increased. Some coordination remained necessary. Some responsibility shifted. What mattered was that the gap was no longer invisible or borne entirely by private effort.

This case shows how sustained engagement can signal need without escalation. By maintaining care within reach and allowing its limits to be seen, participants made a systemic gap legible. Institutional response emerged not as concession, but as alignment with conditions that were already present.

The final section draws these cases together, identifying what they reveal about how engagement interacts with systems when it remains proportionate, visible, and sustained.

Section 5

What These Cases Reveal

Taken together, these cases reveal a consistent pattern. Engagement that is sustained, proportionate, and embedded in ordinary life often produces effects that exceed intention without exceeding capacity. What begins as maintenance—keeping a space usable, making access workable, ensuring care through a vulnerable window—can evolve into something larger when conditions persist.

In each case, action began within reach. People responded to immediate realities rather than abstract goals. The work was practical, bounded, and repeatable. Because it fit into existing routines, it endured long enough to matter.

Endurance changed how the work was understood. What persisted became noticeable. What was noticeable became interpretable. Over time, informal effort produced information about how systems were functioning—or failing—in practice. This information did not arrive as rhetoric. It arrived as condition.

Clarity altered the terms of response. As patterns accumulated, informal adjustment reached its limits. What could no longer be resolved through accommodation entered formal channels—meetings, deliberation, governance. In some cases, institutional response took the form of procedural correction. In others, it required explicit policy or legal clarification.

These cases also reveal the importance of restraint—and its limits. Participants did not begin by scaling prematurely or asserting authority they did not have. Boundaries were respected early on, preserving credibility and preventing burnout. But restraint was not indefinite. When ambiguity persisted and informal correction failed, escalation became necessary rather than optional.

What emerges is a more accurate picture of influence. Influence did not come solely from persuasion or pressure, nor from normalization alone. It emerged from sustained presence that made conditions undeniable—and, at critical moments, from confrontation that forced systems to define themselves.

This does not mean that engagement always produces response. Institutions may still resist. Constraints remain real. But these cases show that sustained, grounded engagement increases the likelihood that systems will first notice, then interpret, and—when required—be compelled to act. Engagement, in this sense, is not a lever. It is a signal—one that sometimes resolves quietly, and sometimes demands law.

The next chapter turns to grassroots organizing—examining how engagement is built, sustained, and escalated in practice, and how people learn to navigate institutions without mistaking early accommodation for resolution.

CHAPTER 10
Grassroots Organizing

Section 1

What Grassroots Organizing Actually Involves

Grassroots organizing begins with proximity. It emerges where people experience a shared condition closely enough to recognize it as a problem worth addressing. This proximity shapes priorities. It limits scope. It determines what kind of effort is possible and what kinds of solutions remain credible.

Unlike large institutions, grassroots efforts operate with minimal infrastructure. They rely on unpaid labor, informal leadership, and borrowed space. Coordination is often improvised. Roles overlap. Knowledge is unevenly distributed. These constraints are not flaws; they are defining features. They shape how quickly action can occur and how long it can be sustained.

Organizing depends on continuity. Momentum alone is insufficient. Efforts built on intensity tend to peak quickly and dissolve. What sustains participation is routine: regular meetings, predictable tasks, and clear points of contribution that do not require constant emotional investment. Endurance matters more than enthusiasm.

Conflict is unavoidable. Disagreement emerges over strategy, tone, risk tolerance, and allocation of effort. Successful grassroots groups do not eliminate conflict; they contain it. They develop norms that allow disagreement without collapse, recognizing that cohesion is maintained through structure rather than unanimity.

Grassroots organizing also interacts unevenly with power. Institutions respond selectively. Some concerns are absorbed; others are deflected, delayed, or reframed. These responses may reflect capacity constraints, competing priorities, or strategic interest in preserving ambiguity. Influence often accumulates through familiarity at first—but familiarity alone is rarely sufficient. When accommodation fails or delay becomes consequential, pressure and escalation may become necessary to force clarity or decision.

Organizing that survives learns to navigate this terrain without confusing early accommodation with resolution, or patience with progress. It adapts its posture as conditions change, recognizing when continued engagement builds leverage and when it merely sustains inertia.

The sections that follow examine these dynamics in more detail—how grassroots efforts form, where they stall or fracture, and what allows them to persist long enough to convert participation into lasting change.

Section 2

How Grassroots Efforts Form and Why Many Stall

Grassroots efforts rarely begin with a plan. They begin with convergence. People encounter the same problem repeatedly and start talking about it in practical terms. Small actions follow—sharing information, coordinating schedules, dividing simple tasks. Early momentum is driven less by ideology than by relief at not being alone.

This initial phase often feels energizing. Participation grows quickly. Possibilities multiply. The effort feels alive. What is less visible at this stage are the constraints that will shape what happens next.

Stalling often occurs when effort outpaces structure. As participation increases, coordination costs rise. Decisions take longer. Expectations diverge. Without agreed norms or processes, friction accumulates. What once felt flexible begins to feel uncertain or burdensome.

Another common point of stall is uneven load. A small number of people often carry a disproportionate share of responsibility. Their reliability sustains the effort, but it also creates fragility. When these individuals burn out or step back, continuity suffers.

Grassroots efforts also stall when purpose becomes diffuse. As new participants join, priorities multiply. What began as a shared response to a specific condition expands into broader ambition. Without clear boundaries, effort fragments. Disagreement intensifies not because people are opposed, but because direction has become unclear.

External response can contribute to stalling as well. When institutions delay, deflect, or partially absorb demands, momentum falters. Participants may interpret this as failure or dismissal. Sometimes these responses reflect misaligned timelines or limited capacity. In other cases, delay functions strategically—preserving ambiguity, avoiding cost, or deferring accountability. Without preparation for either possibility, engagement erodes.

Importantly, stalling is not the same as collapse. Many efforts pause, contract, or reconfigure before stabilizing. Treating these moments as terminal discourages adaptation. Treating them as signals allows groups to adjust structure, scope, posture, or pace.

Understanding why efforts stall is essential for endurance. When stalling is recognized as a predictable phase rather than a personal failure, groups are better positioned to respond constructively—deciding whether to consolidate, escalate, renegotiate purpose, or step back. The next section examines what happens when grassroots efforts encounter institutions directly, and how those interactions shape whether engagement dissipates, escalates, or persists.

Section 3

When Grassroots Efforts Meet Institutions

The interaction between grassroots efforts and institutions is often uneven. Institutions operate with different incentives, timelines, and constraints. Decision-making is formalized. Risk is managed conservatively. Responsibility is distributed across roles and procedures. Grassroots efforts, by contrast, are immediate, relational, and adaptive. When these worlds meet, friction is common.

This friction takes different forms. In some cases, institutional delay reflects limited capacity or competing priorities. In others, delay functions as resistance—preserving ambiguity, avoiding cost, or deflecting responsibility. From the outside, these behaviors may look similar. Their effects are not.

Grassroots groups that endure learn to interpret these signals accurately. They distinguish between delay that signals overload and delay that signals refusal. This judgment is not intuitive. It develops through repeated interaction, documentation, and attention to outcomes—not tone. When familiarity produces movement, patience is effective. When familiarity produces stasis, escalation becomes necessary.

Visibility alone is not sufficient. Consistent, legible engagement helps institutions understand an issue. But understanding does not guarantee response. Institutions act when inaction becomes more costly than action—politically, administratively, or legally. Grassroots efforts that persist long enough often create this shift, whether intentionally or not.

At this point, engagement changes character. Issues move from informal interaction into meetings, deliberation, and governance. Confrontation becomes institutional rather than interpersonal. What is at stake is no longer accommodation, but definition—who has authority, where responsibility lies, and what rules will apply.

Institutional interaction reshapes grassroots efforts in turn. Formal recognition can stabilize an effort by granting access to resources or authority. It can also constrain it, introducing compliance requirements and shifting responsibility. Independence may preserve flexibility; formalization may secure durability. These trade-offs are unavoidable and must be navigated deliberately.

Progress is not always incremental. In some cases, alignment and small adjustments are sufficient. In others, ambiguity persists until it is resolved through explicit policy or law. Resolution, when it occurs, often feels abrupt—not because change was sudden, but because the groundwork was laid over time.

Understanding this dynamic prevents misinterpretation. Grassroots engagement is not a single encounter, nor is patience always the appropriate response. Institutions are environments to be navigated and actors to be challenged. Effective organizing recognizes when each posture is required.

The final section examines what allows grassroots efforts to endure across these interactions—how continuity is maintained when energy fluctuates, conflict intensifies, and outcomes remain uncertain.

Section 4

What Allows Grassroots Efforts to Endure

Grassroots efforts endure when they remain proportionate. When ambition expands faster than capacity, strain follows. Enduring efforts match scope to available energy, adjusting goals rather than demanding constant growth. This proportionality preserves participation over time.

Endurance also depends on role flexibility. People's availability changes. Skills shift. Life intervenes. Efforts that allow roles to rotate and responsibilities to redistribute adapt more easily than those dependent on fixed leadership or singular expertise.

Boundaries are another stabilizing factor. Clear limits on time, responsibility, and expectation prevent burnout. They also protect relationships by making disengagement possible without guilt. Participation that can pause is more likely to return.

Learning is cumulative. Groups that retain knowledge—through shared documentation, informal mentoring, or routine reflection—avoid repeating early mistakes. Continuity improves when insight is held collectively rather than residing with a few individuals.

Endurance benefits from selective engagement with institutions. Some interactions provide support and legitimacy. Others drain capacity. Durable efforts choose these engagements carefully, aligning with institutions where purpose is supported and maintaining distance where it is not.

Finally, endurance requires acceptance of uneven progress. Periods of visibility alternate with quiet maintenance. Outcomes appear and recede. Efforts that persist treat these cycles as normal rather than as verdicts on success.

Grassroots organizing is not sustained by constant urgency. It is sustained by design, restraint, and shared responsibility.

With this foundation in place, the next chapter extends the focus beyond grassroots endurance, examining how engagement continues to evolve as responsibility, scope, and context change.

CHAPTER 11
A Change-Maker's Guide

A Change-Maker's Guide

Section 1

A Capacity-Focused Self-Assessment

Effective engagement begins with an honest assessment of capacity. This is not a question of motivation or values. Many people care deeply about multiple issues. Capacity assessment asks a different set of questions: How much time, attention, and emotional energy are available under current conditions? How variable are these resources? What demands are already in place, and which are non-negotiable?

Capacity is shaped by context. Work schedules, family responsibilities, health, financial pressure, risk exposure, and community ties all affect what can be sustained. These factors change over time, sometimes abruptly. An accurate assessment reflects present conditions rather than idealized versions of availability or resilience.

Overestimating capacity is a common source of disengagement—and a common tactic of burnout. When effort exceeds what can be maintained, participation becomes fragile. Fatigue accumulates. Frustration grows. Eventually, withdrawal feels necessary. This pattern is often misread as a loss of commitment or resolve, when it is more accurately a mismatch between scope and capacity—sometimes accelerated by external pressure or exhaustion.

A capacity-focused assessment avoids this trap. It begins by identifying limits without treating them as shortcomings. Limits are constraints to design around, not obstacles to overcome through willpower. Engagement that respects limits preserves agency, allowing individuals to remain involved without becoming depleted or easily removed from participation.

This assessment also considers tolerance for uncertainty, conflict, and risk. Some forms of engagement involve ambiguity, disagreement, slow progress, or exposure to scrutiny. Others are more bounded and predictable. Understanding which conditions are manageable is not a matter of courage, but of fit. Sustainable engagement aligns effort with temperament, resources, and risk tolerance.

Capacity assessment is not a one-time exercise. As circumstances change, capacity shifts. Periodic reassessment allows engagement to adjust without disengaging entirely. It supports continuity by making recalibration normal rather than reactive—especially when external conditions become more volatile or hostile.

This approach reframes engagement as a practice rather than a test. Participation does not require maximum output or constant visibility. It requires appropriate fit over time. When capacity is assessed honestly and revisited regularly, engagement becomes steadier, more strategic, and harder to extinguish.

The next section examines how scope is aligned before choosing a cause—how decisions about focus protect capacity, preserve leverage, and increase the likelihood that engagement will endure.

Section 2

Aligning Scope Before Choosing a Cause

Choosing a cause often comes before defining scope. This sequence creates strain. When people commit to issues based on urgency, visibility, or moral pull without first clarifying scope, engagement expands quickly and becomes difficult to sustain. Scope alignment reverses this order. It defines the shape and limits of contribution before determining where that contribution is applied.

Scope answers practical questions. How much time can be offered regularly rather than episodically? What level of responsibility is manageable without constant escalation? Is contribution best made individually, collaboratively, or within an existing organization? These constraints narrow the field of viable engagement without diminishing its significance.

Aligning scope protects capacity—and preserves agency. It prevents commitments that depend on perpetual urgency, emotional intensity, or constant availability. Engagement remains bounded, predictable, and repeatable. This steadiness supports learning, coordination, and credibility, even when progress is slow or contested.

Scope also clarifies expectations. When boundaries are explicit, participation becomes easier to coordinate. Others know what can be relied on and what should not be assumed. This reduces friction, limits misalignment, and prevents the quiet accumulation of obligation that often precedes burnout or withdrawal.

Importantly, scope alignment does not require minimizing concern. Caring deeply does not obligate maximal involvement. Engagement gains effectiveness when effort is proportionate to capacity and sustained over time. Modest contributions, maintained consistently, often exert more influence than ambitious commitments that collapse under pressure.

Scope alignment also enables strategic flexibility. As circumstances change, scope can be adjusted without abandoning engagement entirely. Narrowing focus, shifting roles, or reducing intensity becomes a recalibration rather than a retreat. This adaptability allows participation to persist through periods of conflict, delay, or heightened risk.

By aligning scope before choosing a cause, engagement begins with clarity rather than coercion. This approach resists pressure to overextend, protects participants from being exhausted or sidelined, and creates conditions in which escalation—when necessary—can be deliberate rather than desperate.

The next section examines how contribution can occur without overextension—how effort is offered in ways that preserve capacity while remaining meaningful and effective.

Section 3

Contributing Without Overextension

Contribution is often equated with effort. More hours, more responsibility, and more visibility are taken as signs of commitment. While intensity can be useful in short bursts, it is a poor foundation for sustained engagement. Overextension erodes reliability, even when motivation remains high—and in contested environments, it often accelerates disengagement rather than impact.

Sustainable contribution is defined by repeatability. Effort that can be offered consistently—even in modest amounts—creates stability. Others can plan around it. Work accumulates. Learning carries forward. Contribution becomes dependable rather than episodic, increasing its value over time.

Overextension often arises from unclear boundaries. When roles are loosely defined or expectations remain implicit, effort expands by default. Requests multiply. Urgency becomes normalized. Saying no feels personal rather than procedural. Without explicit limits, contribution becomes reactive and difficult to manage.

Clarifying boundaries protects engagement. This includes defining what can be offered, when it can be offered, and under what conditions it may change. Boundaries make participation transparent. They reduce guilt and resentment by aligning expectation with capacity, and they prevent escalation from becoming compulsory rather than deliberate.

Contribution without overextension also requires attention to recovery. Rest is not disengagement. It is maintenance. Periods of reduced involvement allow capacity to regenerate without severing connection. When rest is planned rather than forced, participation is more likely to resume—and less likely to collapse under pressure.

It is also important to distinguish responsibility from obligation. Responsibility is chosen, bounded, and revisable. Obligation accumulates quietly and resists adjustment. When contribution shifts from responsibility to obligation, sustainability declines. Engagement becomes brittle, making participants easier to exhaust, replace, or marginalize.

Contributing without overextension does not mean avoiding challenge. It means selecting challenges that can be met without exhausting capacity or eroding autonomy. Difficulty can be absorbed when effort is proportionate and supported.

Over time, contribution remains effective not because it is maximal, but because it remains possible.

The next section examines how coordination can occur without increasing strain—how people work together in ways that distribute effort, preserve capacity, and prevent concentration from becoming a point of failure.

Section 4

Coordinating Without Increasing Strain

Coordination is meant to reduce effort, not add to it. When coordination becomes complex or rigid, it can consume more energy than the work itself. Meetings multiply. Communication fragments. Decisions stall. What was intended to support engagement begins to exhaust it—and in contested environments, over-coordination can become a point of failure rather than support.

Effective coordination is lightweight. It prioritizes clarity over completeness. Roles are defined just enough to prevent duplication and confusion. Communication is regular but contained. Systems exist to support action, not to document it exhaustively or centralize control.

One source of strain is unnecessary centralization. When too much responsibility flows through a single person or small group, coordination becomes a bottleneck. Decisions slow. Pressure concentrates. Centralization also creates vulnerability—individuals become targets for burnout, removal, or external pressure. Distributing responsibility through shared ownership of tasks or rotating roles keeps effort moving without concentrating strain or risk.

Another source of strain is ambiguity. Unclear expectations force people to guess what is needed or when they should act. This uncertainty increases cognitive load and emotional friction. Simple agreements about timing, response expectations, and decision authority often reduce strain more effectively than additional planning or oversight.

Coordination also benefits from default settings. Regular schedules, standing check-ins, and shared tools reduce the need for constant negotiation. When coordination becomes predictable, it requires less attention. Participants can focus on contribution rather than logistics—and systems become easier to maintain under stress.

Importantly, coordination should remain adjustable. As participation changes, coordination must change with it. Systems that can only scale up become burdensome and brittle. Allowing coordination to simplify as well as expand preserves flexibility and prevents process from outlasting purpose.

Coordinating without increasing strain requires restraint. Not every issue needs group input. Not every decision needs consensus. Choosing deliberately when to coordinate—and when not to—protects capacity, preserves autonomy, and prevents coordination from becoming a substitute for action.

Well-designed coordination distributes effort, limits exposure, and preserves momentum. It allows people to work together without constant synchronization, enabling participation to continue even when visibility decreases or conditions become more demanding.

The final section examines how engagement adjusts over time without disengaging—how participation is recalibrated as circumstances change, pressure shifts, and capacity fluctuates, while connection and purpose are maintained.

Section 5

Adjusting Engagement Without Disengaging

Engagement changes over time. Capacity shifts. Priorities evolve. Circumstances intervene. When engagement is treated as a fixed commitment, these changes are interpreted as failure. When it is treated as a practice, adjustment becomes normal rather than disruptive.

Adjustment preserves continuity. Reducing intensity, narrowing scope, or pausing specific activities does not negate engagement. It reflects responsiveness to changing conditions. Effort that can adapt remains connected even when its form changes, preserving presence without demanding constant output.

Disengagement often occurs when adjustment is delayed. When people push past limits or avoid recalibration out of obligation, participation becomes brittle. Eventually, withdrawal happens abruptly. What appears as disengagement is often the result of insufficient adjustment earlier on—when smaller changes could have preserved continuity.

Making adjustment explicit protects relationships and coordination. When changes in availability or focus are communicated clearly, effort can be redistributed and expectations revised. This prevents confusion, resentment, or silent accumulation of strain. Adjustment, when visible, allows collective work to continue without disruption.

Adjustment also allows learning and leverage to carry forward. People who remain connected at a lower level retain context, relationships, and insight. When capacity increases again, re-engagement is easier and more effective. Knowledge does not have to be rebuilt from scratch, and momentum is not lost entirely.

Importantly, adjustment does not require moral justification. Participation is not a test of commitment or resolve. It is a practical contribution made under real constraints. Engagement that demands constant explanation or apology discourages honesty and accelerates withdrawal. When adjustment is normalized, transparency improves and participation becomes more resilient.

Adjustment is not retreat. It is a way of conserving capacity so that engagement can continue across longer arcs, including periods of heightened pressure or conflict. The ability to scale down deliberately is often what makes later escalation possible without collapse.

Sustained engagement depends on this flexibility. People contribute across seasons of life, not at a constant rate. Efforts that accommodate this reality retain participants longer and benefit from accumulated experience rather than repeated turnover. Engagement endures when it can bend without breaking.

This guide does not prescribe a path or define success. It offers tools for deliberate engagement—tools that allow participation to persist without exhaustion, disillusionment, or quiet removal under pressure.

The next chapter steps back to reflect on the broader arc of engagement—how sustained contribution shapes both individuals and the communities they inhabit over time.

CHAPTER 12
From Practice to Perspective

FROM PRACTICE TO PERSPECTIVE

Sustained engagement changes more than outcomes. Over time, it alters how people understand their place within larger systems—how they interpret delay, uncertainty, resistance, and partial progress. What begins as participation gradually becomes orientation: a way of reading conditions, incentives, and limits without confusion or false expectation.

This chapter considers that shift. After attention, effort, coordination, and adjustment have become routine, something else emerges: a steadier relationship to responsibility and consequence. Engagement is no longer driven by urgency or identity, but by continuity across time. Action becomes less reactive and more deliberate, shaped by experience rather than expectation.

Perspective develops slowly. It forms through repeated exposure to limits, compromise, conflict, and imperfect results. Expectations recalibrate. The desire for certainty softens—not because uncertainty is acceptable, but because it is familiar. Meaning is no longer sought solely in resolution, but in sustained presence where resolution is delayed, contested, or denied.

This perspective is not resignation. It does not require faith in systems or comfort with injustice. It is clarity without illusion. Those who remain engaged long enough learn to distinguish between delay and refusal, compromise and capture, progress and deflection. They act with fewer fantasies about cooperation and fewer misinterpretations of resistance.

What engagement produces internally is neither dramatic nor abstract. It is a way of seeing that resists discouragement without requiring optimism. It allows people to continue participating without mistaking endurance for passivity or escalation for failure. Responsibility is carried with less self-deception and less urgency—but not with less resolve.

This is not a justification for action, nor a substitute for it. It is a consequence of staying present long enough to understand how systems actually behave—and what they require in response. Perspective does not make engagement easier. It makes it steadier. The work continues, not because outcomes are guaranteed, but because clarity has replaced illusion—and participation remains possible without surrendering agency.

Section 1

Belief as Orientation

Belief shapes how people relate to effort. It influences what is noticed, how setbacks are interpreted, and whether engagement remains tolerable when outcomes are uncertain, delayed, or contested. In this sense, belief functions less as a source of motivation and more as a point of orientation—a way of situating oneself within ongoing conditions rather than predicting results.

Psychological research suggests that expectations influence persistence and attention. People who believe effort is meaningful tend to remain engaged longer—not because belief produces outcomes directly, but because it shapes how uncertainty, resistance, and partial progress are interpreted over time.

This distinction matters. Belief does not replace structure, coordination, or action. It does not override incentives, interests, or power. It does not guarantee fairness or response. What it does is shape how individuals inhabit those realities without becoming disoriented, cynical, or prematurely exhausted.

When belief remains grounded—open to revision and informed by experience—it supports endurance without illusion. It allows people to continue acting without requiring reassurance, moral validation, or visible success. Belief of this kind does not insist that systems will respond, only that participation remains coherent even when they do not.

Seen this way, belief is not something to cultivate or defend. It is not optimism, conviction, or certainty. It is a settled orientation that develops gradually through practice—shaped by what engagement actually demands, what resistance looks like in practice, and what persistence requires to remain possible.

Belief that endures is quiet. It does not promise outcomes. It stabilizes attention. It allows effort to continue without distortion—neither inflated by hope nor crushed by delay.

The next section examines how meaning emerges not as a prerequisite for engagement, but as a byproduct of persistence across time, pressure, and imperfect conditions.

Section 2

Meaning as a Byproduct of Persistence

Meaning is often treated as a prerequisite for engagement. People look for clarity, inspiration, or conviction before committing effort. When these are absent, participation feels premature or hollow. Over time, this expectation delays engagement indefinitely, placing emotional readiness ahead of action.

Experience suggests a different sequence. Meaning more often emerges through persistence. It develops as people remain involved long enough to observe patterns, limits, resistance, and consequence. What once felt abstract becomes situated. What felt urgent becomes contextualized. Understanding deepens not through resolution, but through continued exposure to how effort actually functions within a system.

This shift alters how effort is interpreted. Setbacks no longer automatically signal futility. They are read in relation to longer trajectories rather than isolated outcomes. Partial progress feels less deceptive when it is understood as cumulative rather than conclusive. Engagement becomes tolerable—not because outcomes are assured, but because expectations have adjusted to reality.

Persistence also reshapes identity. Rather than defining oneself primarily by positions, affiliations, or beliefs, people come to identify with practices—showing up, maintaining, adjusting, escalating when necessary, and continuing when continuation remains justified. This orientation is quieter and more stable. It does not rely on constant affirmation or visible success.

Meaning that develops this way is less brittle. Because it is grounded in experience rather than aspiration, it does not depend on validation, recognition, or moral certainty. It holds under ambiguity. It survives disagreement. It remains intact when efforts are resisted, delayed, or only partially realized.

Importantly, this form of meaning does not sanctify endurance. Persistence is not inherently virtuous, nor is it justified at all costs. Meaning emerges only when effort remains proportionate, responsive, and capable of revision. When conditions change, persistence that ignores harm, futility, or capture loses coherence rather than gaining depth.

Seen this way, meaning is not something to pursue directly. It arises as a consequence of staying engaged long enough to understand what engagement demands, what it costs, and when it must change form. Over time, this understanding becomes its own source of steadiness—not because it comforts, but because it clarifies.

The next section examines how this perspective reshapes the relationship to success and failure—how outcomes are evaluated when engagement is measured across time rather than moments.

Section 3

Seeing Engagement Over Time

Perspective changes how engagement is evaluated. When effort is viewed moment to moment, outcomes dominate attention. Wins feel decisive. Losses feel terminal. Energy rises and falls with visibility, response, and recognition. Over time, this oscillation becomes difficult to sustain and easy to manipulate.

A longer view alters the frame. Engagement is no longer judged solely by immediate results, but by continuity across changing conditions. Success becomes the ability to remain oriented—adjusting scope, pace, and method without severing connection. Failure is not disagreement or delay, but collapse into withdrawal, rigidity, or illusion.

This perspective softens certainty without erasing judgment. Positions become less absolute. Expectations recalibrate. People learn to distinguish between what can be influenced now, what requires patience, and what may remain contested or unresolved. Engagement continues without the demand for closure—and without surrendering agency.

Seeing engagement over time also clarifies responsibility. Responsibility is no longer experienced as pressure to resolve everything within reach. It becomes attentiveness to what can be maintained, repaired, clarified, or handed forward. Contribution is measured by care taken with conditions, not by scale, speed, or recognition.

This way of seeing does not diminish urgency when urgency is warranted. It contextualizes it. Urgency becomes episodic rather than permanent. Action accelerates when conditions require it and decelerates when sustainability demands restraint. Judgment improves because response is matched to reality rather than driven by momentum, outrage, or fatigue.

Over time, this perspective reshapes participation itself. People remain involved across transitions. Roles change without rupture. Engagement becomes a stable presence rather than an episodic identity. Meaning persists because it is embedded in practice rather than attached to outcome or validation.

This book has traced engagement from attention to action, from individual effort to collective practice, from friction to confrontation, from tools to perspective.

What remains is not a prescription. It is an orientation—one that allows participation to continue without illusion, certainty without rigidity, and responsibility without exhaustion. It does not promise resolution. It makes continued engagement possible in the absence of it.

Engagement, sustained in this way, becomes less about what is achieved and more about how one remains present to work that does not end—clearly, deliberately, and without surrender.

THE END

www.ingramcontent.com/pod-product-compliance
Lightning Source LLC
Chambersburg PA
CBHW070637030426
42337CB00020B/4055